New Directions
in Biography

ESSAYS BY
PHYLLIS AUTY,
LEON EDEL,
MICHAEL HOLROYD,
NOEL C. MANGANYI,
GABRIEL MERLE,
MARGOT PETERS,
AND SHOICHI SAEKI

Edited and with
a Foreword by
Anthony M. Friedson

New Directions in Biography

New Directions in Biography

Essays by
Phyllis Auty, Leon Edel,
Michael Holroyd, Noel C. Manganyi,
Gabriel Merle, Margot Peters
and Shoichi Saeki

Edited and with a Foreword by
Anthony M. Friedson

A Biography Monograph
Published for the Biographical Research Center by
The University Press of Hawaii

General Editor: George Simson

Library of Congress Cataloging in Publication Data

Main entry under title:

New directions in biography.

(A Biography monograph)
Edited papers presented at the International
Symposium on Biography, organized by the University
of Hawaii, Honolulu, 1981.
Includes—bibliographical references and index.
Contents: Keynote address: biography and the
science of man / Leon Edel — Literary and historical
biography / Michael Holroyd — Problems of writing
a biography of a communist leader / Phy!lis Auty —
[etc.]
1. Biography (as a literary form)—Congresses.
I. Auty, Phyllis. II. Friedson, Anthony M.
III. University of Hawaii at Manoa. IV. Inter-
national Symposium on Biography (1981 : Honolulu,
Hawaii) V. Series.
CT21.N48   808'.06692   81–16064
ISBN 0–8248–0783–9 (pbk.)   AACR2

Contents

Biography can no longer be content with summarizing archives and calendar-chronology; it has to understand the psychology of the human being and the myths by which we live. There is a constant struggle between a biographer and his subject—a struggle between the concealed self and the revealed self, the public and the private. The task of biographical narrative is to sort out themes and patterns; not dates and mundane calendar events. This task can be accomplished by use of those very devices which have given strength to fiction. In particular, the biographer should keep in mind four main principles: (1) He must understand man's ways of dreaming, thinking and using his fancy; (2) he must learn to be an objective "participant-observer"; (3) he must search assiduously for the deeper truths which motivate his subject; and (4) he must find the ideal literary form for his subject's life.

The nineteenth-century war between literature and history affected biography in many adverse ways. Recently many good biographers, such as Hugh Kingsmill and Hesketh Pearson, have invoked a spirit of reconciliation which pleads for a synthesizing of the skills of the fiction and the non-fiction writer, so as to restore biography as a great and humane endeavor.

Biographers of communist leaders encounter immense difficulties. They are faced with a gigantic myth which they cannot test against the truth because neither the subject nor his associates wish the truth to be made public, and will use State powers to suppress it. Biographers, nonetheless, attempt these obstacles because they enjoy the intellectual challenge involved in explaining to Western readers how the leader and his followers in the other, communist, half of the world live.

Foreword:
Lifting the Barriers

ANTHONY FRIEDSON

"New Directions in Biography"—an ambitious title for a symposium. It savors, perhaps, of the naively brash. "Oh yes," sighs the weary cynic, "and what else is new?" But anyone who reads, and who does not have a dogmatic aversion to biographical writing, would have to admit that there has been an almost promiscuous increase in the field recently; and that the many works published since the turn of the century have introduced approaches and techniques which would frequently have surprised, sometimes shocked, and occasionally appalled past biographers.

With this vital unrest in mind, the board of the Biographical Research Center approved, in 1979, a proposal by Professor LaRene Despain of the University of Hawaii to organize a symposium on the values prompting new directions in biography. Professor George Simson, President of the Center, asked me to direct this, the first international symposium devoted exclusively to biography. I accepted and together with Professor Despain applied to The Rockefeller Foundation for that help which made the occasion possible. In formulating and executing the aims of the symposium, I received invaluable aid from Dr. Despain and Dr. L. W. Koengeter of the University of Hawaii; and cogent advice from Dr. Joel Colton, Director of Humanities at The Rockefeller Foundation.

We decided that the best method was to bring a manageable number of eminent biographers from various countries and fields to Honolulu (a convenient crossroad between East and West) to offer their ideas on the present and future state of biography. The symposium was to be open to the public and to visiting scholars. In order to widen the representation, without the expense and chaos of a conference, we previously circulated a questionnaire among over four hundred biographers in various parts of the world. (See Appendix.)

The papers delivered at the symposium are collected in the following pages. The papers are printed here in the same order as they were delivered. Their topics move from an emphasis on general biographical philosophy—as represented by Leon Edel's "Principia Biographica"—to an emphasis on more special and particular matters, concluding with Shoichi Saeki's examination of one aspect of biography in one region. Obviously, Edel's discussion of biographical principles is well substantiated with specifics, and Saeki's particular deliberations on Japanese autobiography have general implications, but the logic of moving from the general to the particular is as useful as any. They represent perhaps the most crucial part of an occasion which was far more successful than we could have imagined. They, along with the responses to the questionnaire summarized on pages 84–96, constitute our effort to consolidate and evaluate the salient accomplishments of modern life-writers. They are offered as a provocative guide as to which of the new directions may prove most rich.

Again, one's cynic voice sneers that there are certain problems connected with any "new directions." In the first place, some novelties are not so new. One has only to specify some new direction such as group biography to see it become obsolete on the page. The term is new enough that it was not included in Donald Winslow's recent glossary, *Life-Writing,* and old enough to be adequately covered under its classical term: "Prosopography." There we learned that the direction goes back—at least in a crude form—to such multibiographies as Walton's *Lives;* and Margot Peters reminds us of Johnson's *Lives of the Poets.* Then, Foxe's *Book of Martyrs,* Plutarch's *Lives*—examples ancient and modern suddenly clutter our sights and have to be qualified out of the term if it is to remain "new." Margot Peters obviously has such precedents in mind when she allows that group biography is "arguably" a modern form (p. 41)!

But, even if one admits the arguability of what is new, there is a more important second problem with the concept of new directions. Some novelty may not be worthwhile. It may be a dreary trend which will pass; or, what is sometimes worse, stay as a pustular blemish to leave a scar on the face of the genre—a scar which decent biographers may struggle for decades to smooth away. Phyllis Auty looks with regret on the fashionable "hype" biographies which she feels have scarred Western biography lately. Shoichi Saeki is concerned with the excesses of recent pseudo-biography in Japan. And, among the questionnaire responses, one finds some sturdy objections to certain modern trends. These objections are not merely from isolated reactionaries; nor do they apply only to trivial modes of biography, or to obvious perversions. Some, for example, lambaste very respected modes of thought, such as that concern for individual personality which Leon Edel and others find to be the key element in biography since Freud and Strachey. These iconoclasts extend Saeki's ultimate wariness about the "concept of pure individualism" (p. 82). They feel that the emphasis on personality, and on the detailed study of a subject's life which supports it, has too often degenerated into prurient gossip, more concerned with the passing show than with the ultimate pageant of humanity. At this point, the practitioners of personality will retort that all this is too simplistic; that any credo carries its inherent perversions; and that they would be the first to agree with Saeki and condemn those who beget false practices from true ones.

But this brings up a third argument: that a direction which may be new, and even relatively worthy, may carry the potentiality for damaging or stultifying the craft. Consider, for example, the ancient—but once new—notion that mankind can learn, by example, from the lives of others. This idea has, as Manganyi points out, informed good biography from the life-writers of the bible, through Plutarch to Strachey and beyond (p. 52). Most of us would also admit that this *dulce et utile* credo has made for some very dull books. In the hands of the hagiographers, or their cousins, the political image makers discussed by Phyllis Auty, the conjuring of moralistic exempla has led to the formulaic harnessing of biography for religious or social ends. In the hands of writers of what Manganyi terms "laudatory narratives," it has produced the "graveyard lives" which Leon Edel indicts for having cluttered the history and pocked the honest face of good life-writing (p. 6).

Perhaps such reservations have discouraged, until recently, assessments of where biography today is headed. During the symposium, and in responses to the questionnaire, biographers frequently concurred with Leon Edel's judgment that the criticism of biography is niggardly, especially when compared with that of fiction. Some approved this lack, or felt that it does not matter. They see criticism as a separate literary form—a decorative handmaiden who follows, but makes little essential difference to, the biographical household. But others agree with Edel that "we have reached a moment in literary history when time and circumstance summon biography to declare itself and its principles" (p. 5).

Biography, a journal whose major purpose is to define the field of biography, felt that it should "declare itself." The number of biographical titles being published; their different sorts; and the undeniable public interest made it timely to assess, with adventure and care, what directions currently reinforce the genre or which offer themselves to future writers.

Our first problem was selection. We had to find good biographers who represented a variety of cultures and interests. Obviously, a three-day gathering, featuring only seven major participants, cannot represent completely the complex variety of contemporary biography. But we felt that a gathering of writers from different cultures, fields, and schools would be a meaningful beginning which later symposia could continue. We were lucky. We found seven excellent biographers of differing ages, sexes, backgrounds, and persuasions.

In retrospect, we can see that as we set up the symposium, we were reaching for the end we achieved: a *meeting* in the fullest sense. For, from the discussion in Honolulu and the questionnaire responses, there emerged a main unifying direction under which the subordinate "new directions" may be subsumed: *the dissolution of barriers.*

Again, our devil's advocate might intervene and point out that barriers are inevitable in most fields, and that the word "barrier" may be nothing more than a pejorative term for "specialization." And, admittedly, all genres of literature tend perforce to develop special enclaves; a multifarious genre such as biography is especially prone; and the division of a field into defined areas of interest is not altogether unhealthy. Enclaves encourage, for example, the cooperation of highly informed specialists who enjoy confabulation within manageable and well-unified limits. For that matter, the gathering of specialists for our symposium exemplified the benefits of such intense focusses. Leon Edel's special training in literary criticism, Phyllis Auty's political and historical awareness, Noel Manganyi's work as a psychologist—to name only some of the enclaves represented—made each uniquely qualified to bring a special excellence to the symposium.

On the other hand, most felt strongly that specialists need not be blinkered to other fields and that variegation was healthy. Hovering about the reflections of those participating in the symposium and quite explicit in the responses to the questionnaire is a conviction that biographers of different sorts are currently undergoing a healthy tendency to jump out of the various pens in which their special interest has kept them and work towards a more catholic idea of the craft. Interestingly, for example, even those who thought that there was still little consultation between different backgrounds and factions felt that the situation was improving, and that such improvement was essential. And the symposium exemplified both the existence of the barriers and the extent to which it was possible to resolve them. Certainly, we found it difficult to contact writers in some East European and Asian countries —even in less remote countries such as Yugoslavia and Poland. We had, of course, limited time; and the writers in these lands may have been wary of questionnaires in foreign languages from distant institutions. We were not flooded with responses from such countries—even when we were able to find out where to send the questionnaires. Nonetheless, the questionnaire did bring to bear exciting insights from many parts of the world and from many fields in a way which would have been unlikely in previous eras.

And this was even truer of the symposium itself, where the intercourse was less monodimensional and more dynamic. We were able to hear, for example, exciting discussions between Shoichi Saeki and Noel Manganyi as they considered the interaction of biography and cultural identity. Or we could catch different approaches towards the Fabians from the viewpoint of an American trained in literary criticism, such as Margot Peters, and Michael Holroyd, an English biographer who prides himself on being a non-academic writer.

One could go on about the special ways in which the symposium reflected—and contributed its share to—the catholicity of contemporary biography, but it is perhaps of more universal significance to discuss briefly some of the major ways in which the symposium revealed how the lifting of barriers contributed to specific new directions, alluding where appropriate to the papers which follow.

As we look back on the questionnaire responses and the symposium itself, we can perceive that the major renovating forces derive from the lifting of the following barriers: (1) barriers between different cultures; (2) barriers between different social and political dispensations; (3) barriers between the sexes; (4) barriers between different fields and endeavors; (5) barriers of form between different literary genres, modes and tones of writing; and (6) barriers between theory and practice. Let us consider these, and the manner in which the lifting of each contributes to certain new directions in the field.

(1) Barriers between different cultures

Our speakers represented widely divergent cultures. They came from Africa, Britain, France, Japan, and the United States. And those attending, other than the major participants, represented many other countries.

As I said earlier, this was, as far as we know, the first International Symposium on Biography. There have recently been at least two re-

cent conferences on biography in 1979: that conducted by Marc Pachter at the Smithsonian Institute and the symposium on Canadian biography at Wilfrid Laurier University, Ontario, directed by James Doyle.
Both these were conferences rather than symposia and both were specifically directed at the efforts of U.S. and Canadian biographers re-
spectively. Marc Pachter, and James Doyle—who attended the symposium—were enthusiastic about an international gathering, and the
willingness with which biographers came great distances to discuss
their field indicates the urge which modern writers feel to hear from
those writing in cultures other than their own.

There emerged from the symposium two main ways in which biography profits from cultural interchange—the benefits of *identification*
and the benefits of *detachment*. And if, as we shall see, these appear at
first to be contradictory, the resultant paradox conveys the complexity
of a form of writing which must at once be rooted in the understanding
of a subject's milieu on the one hand, and a degree of detachment from
that milieu on the other. This paradox is part of the larger question of
detached empathy which Professor Edel recommends as his second
principle of good biography (p. 9).

The most obvious advantage of cultural interchange, and of the resulting urbanity, is the writer's capacity to understand more deeply the
context of his subject's life; to perceive and comprehend the coen-
tropes of the subject's culture. The need for such an understanding
may seem to argue against intercultural exchange. When authors write
on a subject from their own culture—as, say, when Norman and Jeanne
MacKenzie write on Wells or the Fabians—the understanding should
come with the territory. All that is required of those writing within
their own world is that, culturally speaking, they know themselves.
Such an advantage becomes especially clear when the subject's culture
is an enclave culture, as when Noel Chabani Manganyi describes the
particular struggles of Ezekiel Mphahlele. Manganyi's paper makes it
abundantly and painfully clear that, when the subject is from a minority, the biographer who is an insider has an advantage over one who is
an outsider.

Even such an advantage, however, carries with it an inherent caveat
which argues the need for an awareness of other cultures. The danger
is parochialism, and the remedy is an awareness of the universal context. A biographer's work, however, sensitive, will be less germane if
he has no sense of an ethos outside his subject's. Conversely, written
into the conscience of a great biographer is a world-grasp. So that Leon
Edel, an American, writing about Henry James, a fellow American,

writes with more universal relevance, and hence, more universal appeal, for his understanding of other cultures, and of the significance of
his subject's life and work to those cultures.

But Edel's work on James brings on a second, more insistent, need
for biographers to have a multicultural sense. James was a man who
crossed cultures. He was, at the end of his life at least, an Anglo-
American—and this is to ignore the extent to which his psyche involved the understanding of other European cultures. To know James
as an American, Edel had to know him as an adoptive European, and
vice versa, and this meant understanding the culture of James' America
as well as that of his Europe, and especially that of his England. Each
culture tended to have its own caste system; its own postulations of vitality and philistinism; its own tones; its own codes and so on. James'
work reveals that he knew all this; and his biographer must be as good,
if he is to see the life, and—in James' case, the work—clearly.

The foregoing arguments would seem to favor those writing in their
own culture, with the proviso that such writers have a universal sense.
By this standard, Henri Troyat, for example, would have been advised
to leave his life of Tolstoy to an urbane Russian who would have come
by, through upbringing, what Troyat had to learn in more secondary
ways. But this is where the second attribute of cross-cultural biography
comes in: *detachment.*

Much has been written, of course, on biographical objectivity. The
best modern books on the craft—such as those by Edel and Clifford—
emphasize the need of the biographer to sit above his material so as to
achieve that "greater objectivity gained from the wider perspective"
(Leon Edel, *Literary Biography,* p. 24). When Edel expressed that
ideal, he was discussing the advantage of writing about a dead subject,
but what he said may equally be applied to writing about a foreign one.

To exemplify the advantage of cultural distance, we need only look
at those who have written about a man as contentious and controversial
as Adolf Hitler. Perhaps no modern subject has so inclined biographers
to write—or not to write—from their own cultural biases. We remem-
ber the early coverage—journalistic image-making; the German writers
busy erecting the myth-laden portrait which Phyllis Auty describes as
symptomatic of politically enslaved biography (pp. 33–36); their non-
German counterparts becoming increasingly polemical in their por-
trayal of the Monster of Berchtesgarten. Predictably, these counter-
portrayals were wound to overplay during World War II. And the
problem continued after the war. The non-German writers still, to
some extent, worked under the Vansittartian notion that Hitler was

merely an emergence of the poison inherent in the German spirit—and found it difficult to relate the man to the best in his culture. Except for a few such as Alan Bullock, it was only recently that biographers addressed themselves to the German cultural background in which Hitler grew to caustic malice and pervasive power.

Were non-German biographers, like Toland and Bullock, at an advantage in approaching a subject outside their own immediate culture? Were they enabled to avoid certain insular presuppositions which would have made their view of Hitler prone to self-indulgence? One might think so. And the fate of Hitler biography in Germany for some decades after the war would support such a view. German writers seemed stunned to paralysis. Perhaps some of them found lacerations on their souls too sore to allow an appraisal. And others may still have been at the mercy of the old myth-makers. Yet others, such as Speer, may have been in a bewildered state of self-justification. One is tempted to believe that working outside the culture induces a special detachment.

And yet one must be wary. We have Joachim Fest's monumental and thorough assessment of Hitler's relationship to his milieu to show us that a German writer may understand yet remain detached. And we certainly have the polemically unbalanced work of some non-German historians and biographers to illustrate that writing from outside a culture does not assure detachment.

The ultimate point would seem to be that a writer, whether writing about one from his own culture or not, should have in mind the broad perspective. And modern biographers increasingly believe that the interaction between cultures is essential to help them "learn to be a participant observer"—involved but not enslaved; a lesson which Leon Edel asserts should be one of the main concerns of modern biography (p. 9).

(2) Barriers between different political and social dispensations

As the foregoing discussion makes clear, political and social matters are an aspect of the culture which produces them. Culture may be defined as the patterns and tones of intellect which govern the development of a region. Politics are the group interactions which may be a part of—or even an impelling force in—such development. But political and even social movements may reach across the borders of different cultures. It is, moreover, possible to effect more speedy change in political and social matters than in cultural ones.

Political and social interchange—and the resultant understanding of
the intricacies of different ways of government and living—are as important to biographers as the lifting of cultural barriers. It is certainly
clear, for example, that one cannot understand Hitler without a thorough background in the development of Fascism; in the circumstances
of Germany under the Weimar Republic and earlier; and in the intricate social factors which alienated Hitler and prompted his political
power. It is even quite obvious that some who are not political figures
in the narrow sense—say, Bernard Shaw or George Sand, MacArthur
or Mishima—were moved by political or social concerns. It may be less
clear, but it is equally true, that the life and art of a political maverick
such as D. H. Lawrence had a great deal to do with political and even
more to do with social factors. The best biographies of Lawrence reveal how the progress from the Bottoms to Taos represented a social as
well as an artistic and personal pilgrimage: an only partially successful
attempt to come to terms with the destructive social conditions under
which he was raised.

It is easiest to understand the problems of the biographer in such
matters—as well as the extent to which one may overcome them—when
we consider the political barriers. And here Phyllis Auty's discussion
of the "Problems of Writing a Biography of a Head of a Communist
State" is most germane. Her awareness of the development of the so-
cialist state in Tito's Yugoslavia enabled her to view the president's life
in the perspective of his political aims. But it is not only the lives of
men in politics which depend on an astute political sense in the biographer. Shoichi Saeki, writing on Yukio Mishima, or Michael Holroyd
on Lytton Strachey, must view their subjects in the context of their
times and of the political and social factors which affected their life and
works. And to some readers, the modes of Japanese or British political
or social life will frequently be enigmatic. The biographer must become an urbane moderator standing astride the barriers, so that the
subject's behavior, in the light of the patterns of his milieu, may become intelligible and emotionally credible.

It is important not to be too roseate in regarding the progress of the
modern biographer's attempt to transcend the boundaries of his own
political and social thinking. In both these areas, our recent progress
has been limited. It is especially easy to perceive the rigidity of political
enclaves, because the power which supports them acts in more palpable and sometimes more absolute ways than it does within political enclaves. Phyllis Auty describes the machinery of some of these ways of
discouragement. Her account reveals how political blinkering distorts

the machinery of evidence as well as the ultimate assessment of the
subject. And the social barriers are equally frustrating to the biographer and lead to similar distortion. Faced with class, or ethnic, ciphers,
an author will often fail to understand some aspect of his subject's life;
may, indeed, find it impossible to gather the evidence or information
which would make such an understanding possible. This situation accounts for the sad circumstances whereby, when the enclave is especially tight (when, for example, one is writing on a gypsy or a black
American), biographies will be susceptible either to the ignorance of
writers who don't know the social set-up of their subjects, or to the self-
imposed censorship of those who are prisoners of their own fraternity.
It is symptomatic, and possibly sad in this respect, that most of those
cited by Noel Manganyi as working on black South African figures are
themselves black South Africans.

The above-mentioned barriers are in three areas—the cultural, the
political and the social—where man has allowed the virtue of variety to
become the vice of provinciality and exclusion. They involve a philosophical rather than a formalistic impact, affecting the substance more
than the form of biography. In this respect one may distinguish them
from the more technical cast of the barriers mentioned below. Obviously, however, any rigorous dichotomy between substance and form
would be fatuous here. A distinctive culture will frequently carry with
it distinctive modes of perception and expression. Some barriers are especially difficult to place in the division because their dissolution carries enormous implications for both substance and technique. A typical
area, in this respect, is that of the third barrier which our participants
felt was disappearing to the benefit of contemporary biography:

(3) Barriers between the sexes

Both sexes were crucially involved with the symposium. Two of our
major participants were women biographers, and about a third of those
attending, or responding to our questionnaire were women. Neither
these nor the male participants appeared to start with any strong bias
about who is contributing, or will contribute, most to the development
of the field. But most felt that the recent contributions by women had
been important. They agreed with Michael Holroyd's sentiments in
his response to the questionnaire—where he singles out the contribution of women as important and overdue. He speculates that "there
will be more women biographers and they will do for biography what
women novelists have recently done for the novel . . . they will help to
create an atmosphere where the reader will experience more acutely

and minutely what it feels to be someone else . . . Without being less accurate, biography will become more imaginative" (p. 96).

There have always, of course, been women biographers, and especially women autobiographers. But, as Shoichi Saeki's discussion of the Heian women autobiographers in tenth and eleventh century Japan reveals, these have frequently been dismissed in a patronizing way. Now, however, it is difficult to patronize such writers as Phyllis Auty and Margot Peters, or to escape the extent to which biography in general has recently lifted the barrier of sex. The number and merits of women writers, and of women subjects, is high. And more important, is the unprecedented interaction between the sexes whereby biographers are choosing subjects from the opposite sex. In our gathering alone, we have had, for example, Phyllis Auty on Tito, Leon Edel on Virginia Woolf, and Margot Peters on Shaw. Such signs of a healthy interaction justify those who feel that we are giving more wit to the Phoenix' riddle and that, in the biography of the future, we two being one are it.

(4) The barriers between different fields and endeavors

Biographers have always striven, to some extent, for an understanding of cultures, social and political groups, and sexes other than their own. Recent progress in these areas is merely a dramatic intensification of past achievements. But the way in which modern biography has involved an unprecedented interaction between various fields is even more remarkable and enriching. And the mechanics of this lifting of barriers between fields is manifold. First, authors and subjects come from many more variegated backgrounds than in the past. Second, both authors and subjects are more frequently involved in more than one field. And third, more biographers are writing about people whose contribution is in areas other than the author's own area of special interest.

Until recently, most biographical studies have been written by those trained mainly in literature, history, or religion—or by those who have at least a dilettante awareness in those fields. And their subjects were principally either important literary figures such as Samuel Johnson; or men whose eminence derives from their historical importance—statesmen such as Thomas More, religious leaders such as Cromwell, or military heroes like Mark Antony. Autobiography, the often neglected or disdained step-cousin of biography, has been less confined; it has sometimes abandoned the high seriousness and portentious purpose which such as Augustine gave it, and, as with Casanova or Colley

Cibber, has become the following clown who mocks its hagiographical-
ly ordained relative. And eventually it influenced its elder. In our own
time, especially, there has been a proliferation of biographies by, and
about, those in other fields: actors, dancers, scientists, lawyers, sports-
men, artists, musicians, architects, and, indeed, subjects in most fields.
    This change may have something to do with the frequently dis-
cussed decline in hero-worship. Readers today may be more interested
in fields of endeavor than in those who excel in them; more interested
in the impact of circumstances on people than of people on circumstances. Obviously Norman Mailer's *Marilyn* [Monroe], say, or Mike
Royko's *Boss* [Daley] are more remarkable as creatures of circumstance
than as moulders of Fortune. Perhaps this is merely a derogatory way
of saying that the Aristotelian concept of the *magnanimous man* as hero
has given way to Arthur Miller's concept of the *common man* as hero.
All of which brings to mind Gabriel Merle's commendation of Manceron's biography of a generation, *The King at Twenty,* when he remarks
that "biography also means listening to the humble ones: it has become
a democratic approach" (p. 66). On a more obvious level, biography's
involvement in more areas is partly—maybe largely—due to the recent
proliferation of biographies and autobiographies, and with the attempt
of publishers to interest a wider reading public.
    Whatever the reason, the representation of many fields, and the
greater interaction between different spheres of interest, has changed
biography in many salutory ways. As biographers have chosen subjects
from more fields, they have represented more comprehensively the
range of man's achievement. There is, too, a tendency to treat men
who have excelled in more than one area. As Gabriel Merle suggests, a
man such as Mauriac is an especially complex subject because of his
dual achievements as writer and politician. Finally, modern writers of
biography often bring a second discipline to bear on their work. Many
agree with Leon Edel when he argues for the integration of science and
art: "What gives strength to modern biographers is the science of anthropology, the observation of the social sciences, above all the explorations of the individual psyche opened up by Freud. The 'new science of man' offers biography a new role in literature and in history"
(p. 6). Edel's work certainly exemplifies his own notion. And each of us
could probably make his list of writers who added to the literary skill
essential to good biography the command of another field—history, art,
music, law, mathematics, for example—which governed his or her material into a special and original unity. As we shall see when considering the interaction between genres, the lifting of the barriers between

fields is sufficiently momentous that it bears on form as well as approach and material. The difficulty of distinguishing between matter and form is obvious when one considers history which has both a form and a substance of its own. And yet, in such as Gibbon or Carlyle, the distinctions between the literary man and the historian disappear.

(5) Barriers of form: genres, modes, and tones

The most dramatic—although not necessarily the most important—changes in the art of biography are those which pertain to liberation in form. Those participating in the symposium—from whatever field—frequently alluded to biography's borrowing of techniques from fiction, drama, history, and even from poetry. The use of dialogue, the carefully managed sense of conflict and climax; the emphasis on personality to the point of characterization; the focusing on specific, crucial images; the employment of an eccentric style—such narrative, dramatic, and poetic arts are found at their extreme in writers who write in other genres, such as Virginia Woolf, Norman Mailer, Studs Terkel, Truman Capote, and Tom Wolfe. These techniques have always been more general in autobiographies than in biographies and, as Saeki's discussion of Japanese autobiography shows, it is sometimes difficult to distinguish autobiography from fiction, especially if the book is anonymous. Some purists would deny that some of these works are biography in the strict sense. But liberating practice seems to be defeating inhibiting purists. More and more, lifewriters are borrowing from other genres. And, fittingly, more poets, novelists, and dramatists are writing biographically. Usually, the biography is loose, as in Weiss' *Marat/Sade,* Sartre's *Keane,* Styron's *Confessions of Nat Turner,* or the poetry of Steven Vincent Benet and Robert Lowell and, more recently, the biographical and autobiographical work of Michael Ondaatje. But the writers of such works would probably admit that they have learned much from their next-door neighbors in biography, even if the lessons were sometimes negative ones.

The most time-honored generic barrier among biographers has been that raised especially by Michael Holroyd—the schism between literary and historical biographers. It is a particularly unhappy division because so many of the essential techniques of biography—the solid base of chronology and the punctilious sense of responsibility toward evidence—derive from the grandparent, history. Happily, many of the most responsible and imaginative biographers today, whether trained as historians or as literary critics, agree with what Holroyd commends as Gerhardie's principal aim: "synthesizing the skills of the fiction and non-fiction writer, to heal the division between history and literature" (p. 25).

The closer relationship between biography and fiction may not seem to have been foreshadowed within the tradition as that between biography and history. One can see in works of the past, especially in an autobiography such as Boswell's *London Journal*, that biographers and autobiographers often took walks in the countryside of fiction, but there will always be a wariness built into biographers in this matter. One has only to observe the rather taut response by some good biographers to a fictional technique such as invented dialogue or, on a more general level, their lack of warmth toward the new journalism. But wariness is not necessarily antagonism. Leon Edel in his address (p. 4) and in the ensuing discussions maintained some distinctions between the fiction writer and the biographer, but his exciting speculations on the future of biography, already propounded in *Literary Biography*, indicate incisively his understanding of the value of fictional craft and the narrative machinery through which it might enhance biography.

Perhaps, in the end, the last barriers to go will be those erected from within by biographers themselves. These are multifarious, and often honored through subtle and almost subconscious acceptance rather than through dogmatic argument. The notion of strict chronology; the practice of full-scope coverage of a subject's life from birth to death; the assumption that the extent of description should reflect the extent of event—these notions and others are sometimes limiting to the imagination and sometimes enhancements to it. (The biographers are always in the process of deciding which.)

A dramatic example of the way in which one formal convention of the art has been modified, if not abandoned, is that which assumed in the past that a biography is principally concerned with one subject. Margot Peters, discussing the history and development of group biography, makes it clear that although there have been occasional examples of multibiography in the past, the recent rage in this form of biography represents a lifting of one formal barrier—that which prevents the treating of many subjects—reinforced by other barriers, such as that against a world view and, in her book *Bernard Shaw and the Actress*, the barrier between sexes.

(6) The barrier between theory and practice

To conclude, we may say that the various new directions discussed above represent a general damning of braces and blessing of relaxes which has either caused, or proceeded from, the current renaissance in biography. Biographers today seem more zealous and definite than in the past. There are, of course, hangovers of the old indefinition. There is, for example, the fuzziness in the critical theory of biography which, Edel asserts, "has not yet articulated a 'methodology'," and "has suffered through three centuries from a lack of definition, a laxity of method" (pp. 4–5). Gabriel Merle reinforces this verdict in relation to France where, he says, biography "does not inspire much criticism, systematic studies are rare" (p. 62). Such judgments are frequently to be found in the questionnaire responses from all areas of the world. Nonetheless, as a review editor, I can say that during recent years—and especially in the last year or two—there has been a tendency for the colt of biographical criticism to move into a trot and very recently into an outright gallop.

A second evidence of indefinition is more pervasive and may take longer to rectify. It is to be found in the diffidence of writers. Some biographers—identified as such in the standard reference works, and well-reviewed as writers of one or two good biographies—responded courteously and perceptively to our questions, but felt that they should make it clear that they did not consider themselves biographers. Such modesty implies mysterious and stern criteria for admission to the fraternity. Would the author of a book or two of poems or of a couple of novels feel underqualified to pontificate about his art? One doubts it. Of course the modesty of this "I-don't-really-consider-myself-a-biographer" disclaimer may be a disguised form of wariness. Holroyd and Edel make it clear that biographers have not always had a good image. There are, and always have been, eminent men who don't want their lives to be open books, and who show what Michael Holroyd terms "a deep hostility . . . to the art of biography" (p. 16). Some of those who disclaim the fraternity may, subconsciously at least, be averse to being thought hyenas. Others, though, undoubtedly think of life-writing as a highly demanding and specialized craft which requires a disposition and a training in excess of other literary genres.

Leon Edel makes it clear that biographers have always suffered from this ambivalent assessment. They are essentially a didactic crowd—at worst, gossip in the marketplace; at best, the perpetuators of parable. And this is, perhaps, the most important value derived from the assessment and lifting of barriers: it enables the writer to transcend gossip and achieve a form of humane assessment. The two are distinct. Gossip, however intelligent, is always a mere servant of the perpetrating individual's ego. Humane assessment—the ultimate end of the good biographer—adapts the most salutory vales of the humane individual's ego to the benefit of the species as a whole. The papers which follow are a part of the attempt to resolve the biographer's ambivalence. They are reflections by seven writers who have contributed in different ways to the lifting of barriers, and who have thus helped to define that field which if properly addressed may be, in Strachey's words, "the most delicate and humane of all the branches of the art of writing."

Acknowledgments

The following essays constitute the foundations of the 1981 International Symposium in Biography. They are published with only minor corrections of the texts delivered in Honolulu, and convey the originality and verve of the occasion of which they were a crucial part. But all who have participated in such affairs know that they depend on contributors other than the major participants. And there were many others—especially those who provided us with funds and facilities and those who contributed advice, spontaneous papers and that discussion from the floor which made our symposium an excited meeting of enthusiasts, rather than a pedestrian observance of academic ritual.

I have already mentioned in my Foreword the generous initial aid given by the Rockefeller Foundation. I should like to add my thanks to the following who made the expenditure and labor worthwhile:

Lieutenant-Governor Jean King, for an incisive and warm address of welcome which proved that biographers have an urbanely informed friend in the executive branch of the Hawaii State Government.

Professor Leon Edel, for invaluable advice and a graceful and apt keynote address.

Professor Travis Summersgill, Chairman, and the faculty of the Department of English at the University of Hawaii, for vital participation and comforting social support.

Professor Dae-Sook Suh, Director of the Center for Korean Studies, and the Center's administrative officer, Mrs. Charlotte Oser, for providing us with an appropriate and aesthetic setting.

Professors Norman and Jean MacKenzie, for advice and for an original and painstaking response to the questionnaire which made us regret the more that they were unable to attend in person.

Mr. Charles DeLuca, Professor Marie José and Mr. Michael Fassiotto, Professor Valdo Vigielmo, Ms. Nobuko Miyama Ochner, Ms. Nancy Castle, and Ms. Carol Ramelb for assiduous editorial and publicity aid.

Professor Emeritus John DeFrancis, Professor Philip and Mrs. Betty Jacob, for essential help with social arrangements.

I should like to thank the fifty to one hundred and fifty resident and visiting biographers and students of biography who enlivened the discussions, and, especially, the following contributing scholars who gave informal and spontaneous papers on various topics:

Joel Colton, Director, Humanities Division, Rockefeller Foundation: "On French Biography."

James Doyle, Wilfrid Laurier University: "Biography and Canadian Literature."

Kathleen Falvey, University of Hawaii: "Drama and Biography."

Sheldon Hershinow, Kapiolani Community College: "Biographical Problems in a Study of Bernard Malamud."

Andrew McCullough, Culture Learning Institute: "The Lives of Irish-American Writers."

In conclusion, I should like especially to thank Professor George Simson who, in moments of query and hysteria, was always profoundly reassuring.

Biography and
the Science of Man

LEON EDEL

Some years ago I set down certain notes for a preface to a hypothetical "Principia Biographica." I argued that it was time to discard our outmoded emulation of James Boswell as a supreme model for life-writing. I pointed out that many things have happened in the field of psychology and the social sciences—in what we might properly call "the science of man"—and that these warranted our taking distinctly new directions in the writing of lives. My notes were destined for a volume in honor of an esteemed biographer who was also a friend, Edgar Johnson. But since several years had elapsed and the promised book had not yet materialized* I decided to begin today by reading those particular notes and then adding a series of elaborations and commentaries relevant to the proceedings of our symposium. My earlier text opened with Michelet's famous wish that he might "give voice to the silences of history." *Je veux faire parler les silences de l'histoire.* This was Michelet's wish. But ours is that they should not say too much. An historian of human lives, endowed with a rage of curiosity, does not want to be drowned in a roar of voices. An interminable chronicle of the hours, days, years is no longer needed. The gaps modern biography must bridge are those Virginia Woolf called "moments of being." And what survives can have its own measured eloquence. I once knew an old French scholar who in his youth and passion for English poetry, went on a walking tour through Italy. He sought every landscape, every town, every house mentioned by the Romantics. On the Grand Canal he met a grizzled gondolier who described the way in which Byron threw open his casement every morning and flung gold coins on the stones of Venice—shaking with laughter at the scramble of penury and greed. I once met a man who sat in the same box at a play with Henry

---

*From Smollett to James in honor of Edgar Johnson appeared in May 1981, edited by Mintz, Chandler, and Mulvey, published by the University Press of Virginia, Charlottesville. The notes in question are on pages 1–10. These, together with the new passages and amplifications here published, are copyright © 1981 by Leon Edel.

James. What had he noticed? Few had a chance to be as close to the distancing Master. My informant said "he had one of those faces—a kind of transparent whiteness of the skin—that made him seem blue-shaven." This tiny bit of visual information seemed as credible as the glimpse of an insolent young English poet scattering largesse out of a Venetian window. Tiny moments surface in the great silences. The color of James's blue-shave, the gestures of Byron—moments of existence, moments of things seen and heard, out of which we write some part of the poetry of human lives.

Biography is a noble and adventurous art, as noble as the making of painted portraits, poems, statues. We know how a painter can give voices to an entire wall; and a sculptor, with skill of chisel and eye, can bring durable life to clay. So a biographer fashions a man or woman out of documents, words. Poetry talks in ikons, images and symbols. A novelist, in his omniscience, knows the measure of his characters, out of his passion for all sorts and conditions of human life. The biographer however begins with certain limiting little facts. "How" exclaimed Virginia Woolf when she sat down to write the life of her friend Roger Fry—"how can one make a life out of six cardboard boxes full of tailors' bills, lover letters and old picture postcards?" How indeed? Yet Virginia Woolf was able to construct a singular life by using such facts as she possessed and bridging the silences with the poetry of her observing and constructing imagination. Her biographer friend Lytton Strachey, spoke of his art as "the most delicate and humane of all the branches of the art of writing." No more delicate, I am sure, than verse, or certain forms of drama. Biography, however, has a particular kind of delicacy. It seeks to evoke life out of inert materials—in a shoebox or an attic—records of endeavor and imagination, cupidity and terror, kindness and love. Strachey called the writing of lives "humane," I believe, because it is a refining and civilizing process: it deals after all with strange volatile delicately-orchestrated beings not mythical gods. The ambiguous records are packed with the contradictions of life itself. A biography (as I have had occasion to say) is a record in words of something that is as mercurial and as flowing, as compact of temperament and spirit, as the entire human being. Perhaps this is what Yeats implied when he wrote "we may come to think that nothing exists but a stream of souls, that all knowledge is biography." Is it not true that all that we know, all that we discover, all that we feel, comes from this stream of souls, and from our own soul or inwardness —human stuff and human sagacity. Every step forward or backward in civilization has been a human step. Behind every mask (Yeats again) there has always been a human face.

Not all artists or historians have such an exalted notion of biography. Some feel it to be a prying, peeping and even predatory process. Biography has been called "a disease of English literature" (George Eliot); professional biographers have been called "hyenas" (Edward Sackville-West). They have also been called "psycho-plagiarists" (Nabokov) and biography has been said to be "always superfluous" and "usually in bad taste" (Auden). Nabokov and Auden felt strongly that lives of individuals who were writers cannot and should not be written. The works writers create—the traced imaginations—suffice; I think they would argue no personal gloss is required. The "new criticism" certainly held to this view: the "biographical fallacy" was critical dogma. It is the work not the life, they said, that counts. In using the word "psycho-plagiarist" Nabokov suggests that biographers are individuals who somehow complete their own lives by writing the lives of others. Such identifications might indeed be called a form of plagiarism; the biographer totally immerses his Self in the Self of his subject. According to Nabokov, he seeks to fortify or reconstruct his own ego by using someone else's. Proust said as much of critics: they were incomplete men, he said, who complete themselves with the work of another. Nevertheless, in biography, whatever the biographer's motivations, a work takes its form, for better or worse. And if the work counts, it is like the breath of the human body, and that body counts as well. A writer writes out of his whole physical as well as mental being. I am not sure the work and the life can be dissociated. As Sainte-Beuve reminded us, *tel arbre tel fruit.*

Written lives engender strong feelings. Yet the biographer works within the unavoidable limitations and restraints of which Virginia Woolf spoke. Biography, we must remind ourselves, is a nascent art even though hundreds of lives are written every year. And it is vulnerable. The anti-biography of Nabokov and Auden reflects artistic reticences. Auden's repeated assertion that biography is "superfluous" may indeed have been more than fear of revelations or even a belief in the sufficiency of his own works. He kept few secrets from his readers. There wasn't much to reveal: his homosexuality was known. Perhaps he felt no further dredging was required. Certainly he had read a great many incompetent biographies. Perhaps he was frightened—enough bad lives are published to frighten any great man. And Auden, moreover, was not alone. William Makepeace Thackeray died commanding that there be "no biography." Matthew Arnold did the same. And in our time T. S. Eliot. But Eliot also admitted that "the line between curiosity which is legitimate and that which is merely harmless, and between that which is merely harmless and that which is vulgarly impertinent, can never be precisely drawn." Henry James went much further. He called down Shakespeare's curse on any one who might try to stir his bones. Let us add that Arnold and Thackeray almost succeeded. Their heirs obediently lowered a curtain: they shut all the doors. When the lives were ultimately written, in a later generation, there had been so great a lapse of time that the biographers worked in considerable detachment and distance. To this day we have had no satisfactory life of Matthew Arnold and Gordon Ray's pioneer life of Thackeray became possible only after he created a monumental edition of Thackeray's letters. T. S. Eliot, as I write, is being loyally defended by his widow. In spite of her efforts, certain "vulgarly impertinent" biographies have appeared. Henry James was defended by his nephew and executor. He had also taken personal precautions. He burned his papers in a great bonfire in his garden at Lamb House. Like Dickens, who lit a similar fire at Gad's Hill (as Edgar Johnson tells us), he could not burn letters which had reached other's hands. When his nephew died James's own epistolary genius, like Thackeray's, betrayed him. His life was made possible because thousands of letters had been treasured and saved. We may note that Auden's request in his will, beseeching his friends to burn his letters, is not being scrupulously heeded. To some of them it would seem like burning Auden himself.

The novel, still hardy and in late middle age, seems to have run its course as a form. One wonders whether there is much more to be learned about the craft of fiction, after the experiments of James, Proust, Joyce, Kafka, and the *nouveau roman*. In its three centuries fiction galloped from the epistolary-picaresque to the high-dramatic, through phases we label "romantic-realism" and "naturalism-symbolism." From dealing with the outwardness of things the novel tried to describe "the stream of consciousness"—indulging in angles of vision, simultaneities and spatial form, as if the novel were a camera. But if fiction has, it seems, exhausted experiment, there remains much to be learned about biography. It cannot claim narrative sophistications. It is backward enough still to invoke Boswell as a supreme model, forgetting that not all biographers can know their subjects as a living presence. Nor has life-writing developed a freedom of form and structure approximating the novelist's freedoms: even as it has not articulated a "methodology." There is a book called *The Craft of Fiction* but no such useful book exists for biography. By its very nature biography has been wedded always—and always will be—to the document, to fact and anecdote, and certainly to gossip; and it will have to reckon increasingly with the portentous libraries heaped around modern figures. Also, in opposition to the novel, it may not invent conversation. The world does a great deal of talking—but rarely in biographies. This is biography's greatest limitation. One of the reasons for the enduring charm and force of Boswell is that he recorded Johnson's words and wit, one suspects accurately, because Boswell himself could not have invented such talk. The tape recorder will be an increasingly useful instrument in providing "oral history" for biographers; but the essential character of the art remains unchanged. As I had occasion to say in *Literary Biography* (1957), "the biographer may be as imaginative as he pleases—the more imaginative the better—in the way in which he brings together his materials." I added, "but the biographer *must not imagine his materials.*" Here lies the heart of our problem. A biographer's narrative imagination is fettered by the very nature of his enterprise. He may be judged therefore by the resourcefulness with which he works—within prescribed conditions. Biographers must be neat, orderly, logical, detached, perhaps even finicky in their tidiness—and yet in this very process they must arrive at the elusive flame-like human spirit which delights in defying order and neatness and logic—and endures so many hours and days doing quite ordinary things, the kitchen-work of life.

We have reached a moment in literary history when time and circumstance summon biography to declare itself and its principles. Can it take its place as a primary art form? I would like to think so; and it should summon poets and novelists to attempt the form instead of leaving it (in Strachey's phrase) to "journeymen of letters." Biography has been the wayward child of individual talents; it has suffered, through three centuries, from a lack of definition, a laxity of method. The biographical feeling inherent in man which gave us the vignettes and stories of the Old Testament and the lives of Christ, which guided Plutarch to write his fabled narratives making us party to the passions of the ancient world, has culminated in singularly few masterpieces. Buried within the unexplored narrative forms of biography is an urge to charter a human odyssey. The fabulous and the magical, the tales of man as a creative enigma, give way now to the exactitudes of science. And caught up in a technological society, man tends to feel himself increasingly dehumanized; thus he once more reaches for the lives of others to assure himself of the commonalities of existence. Biography, when it dealt with ancient times, could allow itself freedoms of conjecture; the material was thin; much of it was folk-tale and the biographer had to make his peace with Michelet's silences—the royal grant of wine accorded Chaucer; Shakespeare's second-best bed. The historian of human lives, in his saturation, could allow himself at best an "educated" guess. Like the architect he might extrapolate columns from fragments. Still, biography has lacked the courage to discover bolder ways of human reconstruction. Our times certainly provide wider latitudes.

What gives strength to biographers is the science of anthropology, the observations of the social sciences, above all the explorations of the individual psyche opened up by Freud. The new "science of man" offers biography a new role in literature and in history. It tells biography that it has for too long grasped the "empirical" and smothered itself too much in externals. There have been too many graveyard lives, the panegyrics Strachey mocked. The celebration of worthies is still considered sufficient—at a moment when there has opened for us new horizons which enable us to use both technology and art in capturing extinct lives. The best counsel Lytton Strachey could give to practitioners was that biography should possess a "becoming brevity": that we should emulate French writers of memoirs and lives, like Fontenelle and Condorcet. These compressed "into a few shining pages the manifold existences of men." Strachey's advice relates principally to craft; yet it implies a great deal of insight into the nature of men *within* their manifold existences. Virginia Woolf wrote more than a dozen brilliant essays on biography. In essence they talked of the struggle between the "granite" of fact and the "rainbow" of fiction. She also wrote a fable for biographers in *Orlando;* and a history of the scent of things when (in her highly imaginative way), she adumbrated a life for Elizabeth Barrett Browning's dog. Having written two imagined biographies, one of an androgynous protean human, who takes varied shapes through the centuries, and the other of a canine, she finally wrote the life of the art critic Roger Fry. Her diaries reveal that she felt harnessed to "fact" while her mind struggled for the freedom of her fancy. If we go back two centuries, we find Boswell, the architect of one kind of modern biography, secure in his intimate knowledge of Dr. Johnson, whom he had observed closely for two decades. He boasted that he would not melt down his materials. He wanted the voice of his subject to be constantly heard. "I cannot conceive," said Boswell, "a more perfect mode of writing any man's life than . . . interweaving what he privately wrote, and said, and thought." Splendid, indeed, when one has access to the subject in the flesh! What would Boswell have done with a modern tape recorder: let us imagine him confronting, at the end of twenty years, a house filled with tapes? He would have been forced to melt his materials or be choked by them. Boswell was in any event being ingenuous; his "oral history" had the benefit of condensations from the first. It was imposed by the labor of the tracing pen in the remarkable minutes he kept of Dr. Johnson's aggressive and pungent manner of conversation. No other instrument was available to him. In the very process of writing these minutes (he did not use shorthand) he selected and even at times "melted down" his data. Yet in spite of this, one reviewer complained that Boswell's gold had not been "ingotted."

His doctrine, or the workshop observations of the moderns, hardly constitute a *principia biographica*. Such a *principia,* less formal and scientific than those of mathematics and philosophy, or the anatomies of criticism of our time, might now be set down in a modest way. Let us recognize that the explorations of Sigmund Freud and his successors have created a new province for biographical adventure and knowledge, and a new audience eager to study particular kinds of human nature and the motivations of human achievement. We might enunciate certain principles for those increasingly attracted to the recording and telling of human lives. One would be that the writings and utterances of any subject contain more secrets of character and personality than we have hitherto allowed. A life-myth is hidden within every poet's work, and in the gestures of a politician, the canvases and statues of art and the "life-styles" of charismatic characters. Whole "case histories" could be compiled out of revealed experience, out of what human beings "express"—for we understand so much more now about behavior and motivation. In this way we can draw larger conclusions about an inner life, of which the "outer" life is constant expression. Some such principles come to us from the new psychology.

In recognizing that biography is accorded at present a secondary place in literary studies we may note the continuing vogue of what some critics have called "an age of criticism." Biography deals with so much human stuff that the interest of both the critical and lay reader has resided in the materials and not in their form or manner of presentation. When the media speak of the "Nixon story" or "the Patton story," it sounds as if there were only one story to be told. The "new Criticism" would not listen, when the new biography argued that the

poet is his poem, the novelist his novel. Criticism, singularly self-
centered, refused to understand that a critic is constantly involved not
only in his own process, which he regards with such self-absorption
and often self-indulgence, but in a biographical process as well. The
winds of change can be seen in the curious theorems of critics like
Harold Bloom, who uses Freudian generalizations, and splashes about
a great deal in biography. In this indirect way such a critic is announc-
ing the belated wedding of biography and criticism; but also of biography and psychology—or to put it another way, he announces the
gradual awakening of criticism to the fact of an inexorable and un-
divorceable marriage. Is it not strange that many critics who attempted
to write lives have floundered in the archives? They thought of biography only in Boswellian terms; they felt as if the recital of the classic
laundry lists was what biography really is. The critical ego often is so
deeply concerned with critical ideas and their justification, that it is in-
capable of empathy with the vicissitudes of lived lives. So we are now
in the process of putting the poet back into his poem after trying to re-
move him or drown him in floods of critical explication. We are beginning to understand—what historians knew always—that literary history
is a record of what happens from the moment an imaginative writer
puts pen to paper, or speaks words into an electronic device, or applies
his fingers to a typewriter keyboard. The world's curiosity asks more
insistently than ever for the humanity of the lived life. It wants to
know how poems or stories, paintings or music, politicians or soldiers,
came into being. Strange indeed the ways in which poets themselves in
popular readings of their words, facing enraptured audiences, have
found it expedient to talk of their art, their thoughts, their divorces,
their children. The impersonal poet and his impersonal poem disappear. A whole new land of biography has been opened by "confessional
poetry." Biography seems to be at a threshold. Individuals in our society proclaim their lives from the roof tops. Our greatest problem is to
find artists equal to the task of setting them down.

In these jottings for a *Principia* I find myself tracing four principles
which have been my main theme these many years. I have already suggested two and I will expand them:

The first is that the biographer must learn to understand man's ways
of dreaming, thinking and using his fancy. This does not mean that a
biographical subject can be psychoanalyzed; a biographical subject is
not a patient and not in need of therapy. But there can be found analytic methods applicable to biography in which the subject's fancies,
thoughts and dreams are used for the revelations they contain. By an

analytic approach to biography I mean the kind of analysis which enables us to see through the rationalizations, the postures, the self-delusions and self-deceptions of our subjects—in a word the manifestations of the unconscious as they are projected in conscious forms of action within whatever walks of life our subject has chosen. The very choice of a given walk of life is in itself revelatory. Such analysis is not learned from reading a book by Freud or Jung or the other writing psychoanalysts of our time. The biographer must first learn to understand his own fancy so as not to confuse it with that of his subject.

This brings me to the second principle—that biographers must struggle constantly not to be taken over by their subjects, or to fall in love with them. The secret of this struggle is to learn to be a participant-observer. A good biography implies a degree of involvement—otherwise the work has little feeling. But there must, at the same time, be a strong grip on the biographical self, so that total disengagement is possible. An empathic feeling need not involve identification. No good biography can be written in total love and admiration; and it is even less useful if it is written in hate. This problem of identification is in reality at the core of modern biography, and it explains some of its most serious failures.

The third principle, which might be an extension of the first, is that a biographer must analyze his materials to discover certain keys to the deeper truths of his subject—keys as I have said to the private mythology of the individual. These belong to the truths of human behaviour which modern psychology has extensively explored and which we must assiduously study. This is what I mean when I speak constantly of searching for "the figure under the carpet." By studying first the figure in the carpet—that is the patterns and modes of a man's works, in literature, in politics, in most of his endeavors—we are able then to grasp what lies on the underside of the given tapestry. The public facade is the mask behind which a private mythology is hidden—the private self-concept that guides a given life, the private dreams of the self. In seeking this mythology we use inductive methods as boldly as a detective uses deductive. The ways in which men and women handle their lives, the forms they give to their acts of living, their particular forms of sexual politics for example, their handling of human relations, their ways of wooing the world or disdaining it—all this is germane to biography, it is the very heart of a biography. The rest usually falls into place once we possess this knowledge. The mythological keys help guide us through the mazes of modern archives. But we must also recognize that, while the mythological configuration is more or less determined, there are cases in which we find ego development and ego change. We are, however, constantly involved with determinism.

My fourth and perhaps final principle for this discussion relates to form and structure. Every life takes its own form and a biographer must find the ideal and unique literary form that will express it. In structure a biography need no longer be strictly chronological, like a calendar or datebook. Lives are rarely lived in that way. An individual repeats patterns learned in childhood, and usually moves forward and backward through memory. Proust is perhaps a better guide to modern biography than Boswell.

In sum I would say that my four principles—and doubtless others will come up; these are but starting points—suggest that a constant struggle is waged between a biographer and his subject—a struggle between the concealed self and the revealed self, the public self and the private. And the task and duty of biographical narrative is to sort out themes and patterns, not dates and mundane calendar events which sort themselves. This can be accomplished by use of those very devices that have given narrative strength to fiction—flashbacks, retrospective chapters, summary chapters, jumps from childhood to maturity, glimpses of the future, forays into the past—that is the way we live and move; art can be derived from this knowledge.

Let these four principles stand as my view of some of the foundations of the New Biography: the biography we have been creating since the days of Lytton Strachey. He was the first to use Freud in a constructive manner—although he used him *en amateur* and at secondhand. I would add finally that a biographer who does not possess a literary style and the ability to be concise and clear, had better shut up shop. Brilliant lives have been dulled by dull biographers; and dull lives have at times been rendered brilliant in the same process. A singular part of our quest is a quest for proportion. A life must be shaped, but not distorted or made subject of the biographer's eye. The integrity and intensity of the biographer's process, and his ways of proceeding, usually shine through his work. He is far from anonymous. He is present in his work as the portrait painter is present in his. And he stands or falls by the amount of confidence or of distrust he creates in the reader.

Let me add as a possible subject for our discussions the question of biographical criticism. There exists, I am sorry to say, no criticism of biography worthy of the name. Reviewers and critics have learned how to judge plays, poems, novels—but they reveal their helplessness in the face of a biography. They reflect their uncertainty about the fact, which they can't immediately verify, and so they discuss their own interest in the details or gossip of a life rather than in the art of representation which a biography must be—and it is this art which is truly their concern. Biographers are left with only one course: to teach critics how to read a biography with proper judicial awareness even if the critic doesn't know the archive. How has the biographer distinguished between his reliable and unreliable witnesses? How has he avoided making himself simply the voice of his subject? How has he told his story? Does the data produced justify itself in the narrative? These questions are answerable in the reading of any biography.

You can see from my fragmentary notes for my proposed *Principia* how the problems are intertwined and how difficult our task will always be. Which is why we welcome the initiatives that have brought about our symposium. I hope that it will be but the first of many designed to begin a process of educating the public and biographers themselves in what is still a virgin field. Up to the present biography has been an art little aware of itself and mixed up too much with *ad hoc* rules of thumb, personal superstitions and personal prejudices. We are at the very beginning of our journey.

Literary and
Historical Biography

MICHAEL HOLROYD

For reasons which *may* become apparent, I should like to begin on a
personal note. Whatever I may achieve as a biographer I will owe,
more than to anyone else, to the example of a writer called Hugh
Kingsmill. I never knew him: he died at the end of the 1940s. And by
the time I came to his books, accidentally one day in a library, he had
already been dead for several years. But what I read of his, at about the
age of twenty, gave me the courage—the obstinacy, some would have
said—to continue trying to write. For it was Kingsmill who made literature real for me: who made the connection factually and imaginatively
between what we read and how we live. Most of us have some favourite
under-valued writer: someone whose books we have read at precisely
the right time (timing is vital in these matters) and whose failure to
achieve public recognition affronts us. Kingsmill is that writer for me.
He didn't waste words and in a society that pays by the word he remained poor. But his was an original voice. He belonged to no school
of authors, neither inhabiting Bloomsbury nor contributing to *Scru-
tiny.* He represented an alternative tradition going back, I believe, to
Dr. Johnson. He judged literature by its truthfulness and by its power
to reveal individual truths through humour, pathos, tenderness. He
had a gift for spotting humbug, and his judgements, delivered with wit
and epigrammatic flair, are moralistically intuitive to an extraordinary
degree. What he offered me at that age was not part of the schoolroom
but what goes on outside it: what is felt rather than endured.

Kingsmill believed that most works of history and biography should
be given an autobiographical Preface to enable the reader better to interpret what follows. The same principle, I imagine, also applies to lectures. So, as a Kingsmillian, perhaps I should explain that I have been
a person to whom, all my life, things have not happened, sometimes in
the most spectacular way. I have only to write a letter and almost at

once it seems to me I get no reply; or enter a room and someone opens the door and cries: "no one here!" This may have come about because I was brought up largely by grandparents and took their pace and their condition rather than my own—that is, the regime of seventy- and eighty-year olds when I was seven or eight. To compensate for a passionately inactive life, I filled my head with book adventures. Then, under Kingsmill's influence, I went one stage further, stepping from my own life into other peoples'—where there appeared to be more going on.

My first biography was about Kingsmill himself and I think I may say without boasting that it is not a good book. Kingsmill, unknown before I came to write about him, remained unknown after the publication of my life of him. But although a first book by an unknown writer about an unknown author may not be, in publishing terms, auspicious, it had started me on my way. I had met, for example, my first living biographer, Hesketh Pearson, who had been a friend of Kingsmill's and to whom I wrote asking for information as part of my research. That was one of the letters to which I did get a reply. From Pearson I received constant encouragement over the years it took me to get my first book published. We talked about the writers we liked not as if they were embalmed upon the page, but living people who might breeze in at any minute.

Pearson, I should explain, was a man of strong opinions. One day, when someone made a disparaging remark about Shakespeare, he stopped the taxi they were travelling in and obliged the man to continue his journey on foot. Books were not something behind which he sheltered: they were part of his life and he helped to make them part of mine. If Kingsmill had made literature real for me, Pearson had made it a way of life. His technique of writing biographies, which derived in part from an earlier career on the stage, was different from mine. But I learnt much from him about the organisation of material, about the craft of narrative and about the atmosphere of sympathy, so different from sentimentality, in which characters may be recreated.

And I learnt something about the choice of a subject. Though it is difficult to get writers to agree as to what is a good book, almost all of us wholeheartedly agree that there are too many books. We should have, I believe, a resistance to writing books that only the most genuine enthusiasm can overcome. In the case of Hesketh Pearson, certainly, it seemed that the greater the enthusiasm the better the book. He wrote from a genuine love and fascination for his subjects (which included Wilde, Shaw, Gilbert and Sullivan, Conan Doyle, Sydney Smith) and he produced not hack works but what is called "popular" biography. This description used to make him smile. He was over 50 by the time he was able to live from writing alone. But he had a good library public I believe. In an analysis of his work, Anthony Burgess has written:

> The term *biography* connotes for many of us a kind of life-story that Pearson would not have much relished having to write: I mean the huge professional job, crammed with footnotes, many-paged and very expensive. We need such biographies, and I have many, which are often too heavy to lift, on my shelves. They are necessary works in that they represent final factual authority, but they do not have to be readable. You consult them, but you do not take them to bed. What Hesketh Pearson wished to do, and succeeded in doing, was to produce racy lives of the length of a novel, unencumbered by a professorial apparatus and yet evidently accurate, their scholarship a property that the reader could be seduced into taking on trust. Pearson's biographies are charming and, indeed, heavily seductive. There is a smile in them, but it is not a meretricious smile.

Such work is not to be despised: indeed it is the sort of work that may set alight an unquenchable interest in biography. Here is a distinct category of biography that today is in danger of being fashionably under-rated—especially in our universities which tend to treat biography merely as a system of information retrieval. We must, I suggest, all beware of taking well-researched solemnity, footnoted earnestness, lack of enjoyment itself for seriousness. True seriousness, I maintain, must always contain seeds of humour and vitality. About biographical theories Pearson himself was reticent. Had he been here, he would not have figured prominently in our discussions: he would have been on the beach or in the mountains. "No one should attempt to combine practice with theory," he said during a lecture to the Royal Society of Literature. In 1930 he had published a volume of biographical criticism—but that, he explained, was when "having no practical experience I knew everything about it. Now, after writing the lives of seventeen people, I find I know nothing about it."

One of my own biographical devices has been to use, here and there, my subjects' techniques, attitudes, vocabulary, tricks and manners: and, short of parody, apply them back. But not having written seventeen biographies, I will allow myself a little un-Pearsonian theory. Pearson *acted* his subjects. On the stage, where he had understudied Sir George Alexander, his performances had been remarkably erratic—very good when a subject suited (that is *resembled*) him, and extraordinarily bad when it didn't. In principle, the same is true of his biographical performances: only by that time his instinct had sharpened and he could choose whom he acted on the page. To some extent he "Pearsonified" his characters: they tended to express themselves in explosive Pearsonese. His style had been influenced by Bernard Shaw—it was extremely assertive and had about it an air of epigrams, plus the sound of booming alliterations. His pen portraits are done in primary and effective colours—he is an expert at the job. It is only when you look closely that you can see how solid is the underlying draughtsmanship. Above all, he relished human personality and used his subjects' work as an aspect of that personality. As he understudies one or other congenial hero, he is joyfully partisan.

People knew where they were with Pearson. They read him for enjoyment, eager to find out what happened next, and while they read the atmosphere of the book gathered round them. By the end they felt they knew Hazlitt, Whistler, Labouchère or Tom Paine as they knew someone in the same street. Pearson did not so much take you back: he brought them forward. His treatment was conversational and impressionistic, not analytical: it depended on anecdotes and the dextrous building up of incident to achieve its effect. He didn't bother with dreary documentation, but his use of quotation is extremely deft. Much of his scholarship—or rather *knowledge*—is concealed in the interests of making something vivid. He is cheering—and occasionally infuriating—to read.

The danger of Hesketh Pearson's technique of biography is that each biography may become a form of autobiography; and that in the character-acting of your subject you bend him or her to the demands of your acting skills. Robert Graves suggests this in his poem "To Bring the Dead to Life", written almost as a primer, you might say, for the school of actor-biographers. He wrote:

Subdue your pen to his handwriting
Until it prove as natural
To sign his name as yours.

Limp as he limped
Swear by the oaths he swore;
If he wore black, affect the same;
If he had gouty fingers
Be yours gouty too.

But in another passage from his poem he utters a more sombre warning to such a biographer as myself. It is my belief that, especially in literary biography, the biographer stretches out his hand to his subject

and offers him or her the chance of what amounts to a posthumous
work written in collaboration. The biographer, it seems to me, lives
partly with the dead and his job is, in a sense, to resurrect the dead.
That is why the title of Robert Graves's poem "To Bring the Dead to
Life" appealed to me. But then, of course, the dead may be very happy
where they are. For many writers their work, which may live on, becomes more vital than their lives which must come to an end. Besides,
some of them fear that their lives actually hinder an appreciation of
their work. From the biographer's point of view, however, their lives
may be the raw material of his work. So a tug-of-war may develop in
which the dead are not brought to life but the living pulled into a dead
world. That, at any rate, is one way of reading Graves's poem. It begins with such deceptive ease and ends with the horror of a ghost story
by M. R. James. Here it is:

> To bring the dead to life
> Is no great magic
> Few are wholly dead:
> Blow on a dead man's embers
> And a live flame will start
>
> Let his forgotten griefs be now,
> And now his withered hopes . . .
>
> Assemble tokens intimate of him—
> A seal, a cloak, a pen:
> Around these elements then build
> A home familiar to
> The greedy revenant
>
> So grant him life, but reckon
> That the grave which housed him
> may not be empty now:
> You in his spotted garments
> Shall yourself lie wrapped.

Do biographers change places with the illustrious dead in this way?
Do our bodies risk becoming their coffins or places for their spirits to
inhabit? In such science fiction terms it is easy enough to dismiss these
notions as preposterous. And perhaps they are fanciful—at least exag-
gerated. But the criticism itself is interesting. You would never hear it
levelled at an historian, I believe. And it is impossible to conceal the
deep hostility within it to the art of biography. From what does this
hostility spring? You may see it everywhere: in George Gissing's dis-

missal of biography as "farce", and James Joyce's description of its practitioners as "biografiends". J. M. Barrie spoke for many writers when he uttered his curse on all would-be biographers: "May God blast anyone who writes a biography of me." Most poets and novelists aim their hostility at what they feel to be the imposing irrelevance of those damn thick square books of so-called non-fiction. But other categories of writer fear it too.

Perhaps the most astonishing example of this fear is that of Sigmund Freud. At the age of 29 Freud (like Dickens and others) made a bonfire of his papers. "As for the biographers," he remarked, "let them worry . . . I am already looking forward to seeing them go astray." Later in his life he again destroyed a large collection of private papers: and when he discovered that Princess Marie Bonaparte had acquired his early letters to Fliess, he tried unsuccessfully to buy them back. His published autobiographical fragment is marvellously reticent, and there seems to be no doubt that he deliberately concealed aspects of his early love life. But is there not, in this mixture of reticence and concealment, the beginnings of megalomania? For really it was less himself than his work that Freud was seeking to protect. Like other writers, he felt his work was his immortality—and he laid down his life for it. Reviewing Ronald Clark's excellent biography of Freud, Anthony Storr suggested that "Freud's early correspondence reveals how much of psycho-analytic theory depends upon the subjective emotional experience of its founder rather than being derived from his observation of patients. Freud tried to make out that psycho-analysis was a science, and that he was a detached, objective observer, but neither claim can be sustained."

Other writers too like to claim that their work is, if not a science, a piece of magic. "A shilling life will give you all the facts," stated W. H. Auden at the beginning of his poem "Who's Who". Then he goes on to list those facts and mock the naivety of biographers who feel disconcerted by the ordinariness of the outward life of extraordinary writers:

> With all honours on, he sighed for one
> Who, say astonished critics, lived at home
> . . . answered some
> Of his marvellous letters but kept none.

What Auden purports to fear—and I shall come back to this later—is the eclipse in the reader's mind of all that extraordinary work by all that ordinary experience. The moon is a dead body, having nothing but reflected light: but it can blot out the sun. So it is with life and work. Whenever a writer, artist, musician, any man of imagination is made the subject of a biography, his light may be extinguished. For, the argument goes, life is simply a shell, the kernel of which is creative work. There is no real nourishment in biography. The words fly up, the lives remain below. Words without lives only to heaven go. So jettison the life—that seems to be the fashion. And it rests on the assumption that the biographer values a writer's work only for its autobiographical ingredients. He has the Midas touch—but in reverse. Each piece of gold he touches turns to dross. If you value your work you must not let a biographer near you—that's the popular feeling. Somerset Maugham, George Orwell, T. S. Eliot and most recently Jean Rhys, all seem to have shared something of this superstition. But how valid are the assumptions from which these fears arise? I would like for a few moments to look at the objections of various authors, both in theory and practice, to the writing of biography. To some extent they seem to derive from the writer's wish to have the last word, and for that last word to ring uncontradicted down the ages. It is a very natural wish. We all long for the judgement of history to coincide with our own living testimony. But most of us, I think, do not greatly admire ourselves if we attempt to impose our wishes artificially by posthumous methods. It is better, I suggest, to learn how to rest your case and how to reconcile yourself to the strange acoustics of life where words that leave your lips in the euphoria of blazing truth reach other people's ears as more sombre and complicated sounds.

It is particularly undermining, even dismaying, when non-fiction writers destroy evidence. But they can do it no less efficiently than novelists or poets. We have already glanced at the case of Freud. G. M. Trevelyan is another example. Trevelyan maintained that history should not be what he called "merely the mutual conversation of scholars." He was strongly opposed to what was then the fairly new school of academic historians which wanted history removed from the discipline of literature and the humanities and treated as a science. Trevelyan was a sincere man. J. H. Plumb wrote of him that "absolute integrity and total honesty combined to make him one of the greatest men I have ever met." But Trevelyan found difficulty in embodying his beliefs. He burnt, after her death, most of his correspondence with his wife. He published in 1949 a brief "Autobiography" which provides only the minimal background information to his work as an historian: and he "sternly forbade anyone to write his biography." Did this prevent his daughter, Mary Moorman, from becoming a biographer? It did not. Recently, too, she has published a memoir of her father that draws upon all those letters to his family that had escaped the flames. It is proper that such ironies—affectionate, in this case—should exist: and it is inevitable. They are the commentary of life upon our wishes to tailor existence into some sort of well-fitting straitjacket. Stern words in wills, though embarrassing, are not realistic. Besides, if literature grows too far apart from the vitality of actual life, it begins to wither in its artificial circumstances and to become that scholarly conversation Trevelyan himself had derided. Trevelyan's greatness, as J. H. Plumb records, lay not purely in his work but also in his personal qualities. But they were threaded with a strain of stoical melancholy of which his embargo against a biography may well have been one symptom. It is only just that in her sympathetic memoir, Mary Moorman records Trevelyan's own admission that as an historian he "had been too bookish."

That it is not practical to protest too much has been proved many times over. Just look what happens. Somerset Maugham objected and his objections have apparently made the writing of books about him irresistible. He might even have mildly welcomed some of them—those, for example, by Francis King, or Frederic Raphael or Anthony Curtis. But what about that scandalous little book by Beverly Nichols? There was nothing he could do about that but make it worse. One of the most choice literary ironies was that Beverly Nichols was actually a signatory to Maugham's Will, making it impossible for him, in the usual sense, to figure as a beneficiary. Despite leaving instructions to his literary executor not "to assist any person who wishes or attempts any such publication," Maugham's literary executor Spencer Curtis Brown eventually gave his full assistance to one of the most detailed biographies of the sort Maugham particularly dreaded, by the Pulitzer Prize winning journalist Ted Morgan. And did readers and reviewers indignantly champion Maugham against his impolite biographer? Not at all. They did the very opposite. Anthony Burgess, for example, wrote: "There will, I think, be nobody who will do other than approve Spencer Curtis Brown's decision to disobey the letter of Maugham's instructions. No one can forbid the writing of his life, and it is hence wrong to put obstacles in the way of its being properly done." And this, I should add, was Anthony Burgess's verdict despite his opinion that the biography in question was without literary merit. We can see other examples that support this argument in the case of T. S. Eliot. Perhaps because of Eliot's embargo, directly or indirectly, that master biographer Richard Ellmann did not write Eliot's Life. Instead we had the sympathetically initialled Mr. T. S. Matthews of *Time* magazine; and we also had the late Robert Sencourt's dreadful book. Nothing could have been further from Eliot's wishes; but it was those wishes, ironically, that made the opportunity. The point I am making is that those who fear biography are often the same people who make it fearful.

Among the most fearful of all, as we have seen, are some poets. To illustrate this I must again break Holroyd's Rule—which is never, *under any circumstances,* to read a poem in a lecture. So here is a poem called, simply, "Biography" written by D. J. Enright.

> Rest in one piece, old fellow
> May no one make his money
> Out of your odd poverty
>
> Telling what you did
> When the sheets stared blankly back
> And the ribbon fell slack
>
> The girls you made
> (And, worse, the ones you failed to)
> The addled eggs you laid
>
> Velleities that even you
> Would hardly know you felt
> But all biographers do
>
> The hopes that only God could hear
> (that great non-tattler)
> Since no one else was near
>
> What of your views on women's shoes?
> If you collected orange peel
> What *did* you do with the juice?
>
> Much easier than your works
> To sell your quirks
> So burn your letters. hers and his—
> Better no Life at all than this.

That poem is good in that it brings together neatly and succinctly and wittily, and indeed with feeling, so many of the prejudices surrounding biography. It presents biographers as writing their books from a variety of motives, all of them pretty sordid. They write for money—and worse they get money while the poet remains oddly poor (his treasure being in heaven). Biographers are know-alls; they seize on the irrelevant;

they reduce life to gossip. They parody the poet. Far from being real writers they are saboteurs within the ranks of real writers.

No biographer would deny that there are many bad biographies written and that some of them may be written to one or other of these formulas. But then (you have only to see them at one another's throats) no poet would deny that there is a good deal of bad poetry written too. That of course does not invalidate all poetry. It is perhaps more of an indictment against publishers—which reminds me that D. J. Enright is, as well as being a poet, a publisher. Where I think his poem may be sentimental is in its impressive sweepingness—and in its implication that poets, in the heights of their inspiration, are above biography which should only record action. The assertion against biographers is that they play God; but the accusation against poets is very similar. We have an embarrassing amount in common.

It may be perhaps because they feel they have more to lose that poets have always been among the more extreme critics of biography: and, as the case of T. S. Eliot shows, they have often fared badly at the hands of biographers. Who can doubt that W. H. Auden's sanctions against modern biography have given the book on him by his friend Charles Osborne a lurid addition of publicity? Examine what Auden wrote in the foreword to his last anthology *A Certain World.* "Biographies of writers," he wrote, "whether written by others or themselves, are always superfluous and usually in bad taste. A writer is a maker, not a man of action . . . [and] no knowledge of the raw ingredients will explain the peculiar flavour of the verbal dishes he invites the public to taste: his private life is, or should be, of no concern to anybody except himself, his family and his friends." Then, after saying that he was writing this into his Will, Auden added: "And I am asking all my friends to destroy any letters they have from me." The impracticability of this scheme we need not labour: in the shop windows there is Charles Osborne's handsome book to illustrate it. But it is always a dangerous sign when someone, especially perhaps a poet, begins to tell everyone what they "should" or should not be feeling, thinking, doing. Auden assumes too that the justification of literary or artistic biography must lie in its value as illuminating criticism of the work. That is not so, and at other moments Auden knew this. He is bewilderingly, sometimes delightfully, inconsistent. What a lot of biography and autobiography he read and how his reaction to it varied! It is surely extraordinary that someone so antipathetic to the lives of writers should have written quite so many autobiographical poems; or that someone so apprehensive of the lives of homosexual writers, should speculate in such detail about A. E. Housman's homosexuality or complain that, in his autobiography *My Father and Myself*, J. R. Ackerley had never been "quite explicit about what he *really* preferred to do in bed." In this context Auden wrote that "all 'abnormal' sex-acts are rites of symbolic magic." But whenever he linked the idea of literary biography to himself he became hostile—there were too many complicated and unhappy incidents in his life. Richard Ellmann has to my mind convincingly explained that for various reasons "Auden felt uneasy about having anyone else manipulate the entrails of his experience. Of course they would not get it right. But besides that, he had a well-developed sense of guilt. He did not feel that he had spent his life in the way he ought to have done, and was conscious of much that might be revealed to his discredit. He disliked evasion, but he had evaded. He disliked pretensions, but he had pretended. He disliked imperfection, but was conscious of having too often 'slubbered through/with slip and slapdash what I do'."

In view of all this, it is encouraging to add that it is Auden who, in another context, gives the real justification for biography when he writes: "A work of art is not *about* this or that kind of life: it has life." That, of course is what the best biography has. If it is a form of resurrection (where the biographer risks being absorbed into a dead world), it is not primarily the resurrection of a reputation—that indeed may well be superfluous to the vitality of biography. To take an obvious instance: the length of a biography does not reflect the importance of its subject (a ludicrous though popular notion): it reflects the interest of the material available and the effect that material has produced on the mind and feelings of the biographer. That is all.

If, in speaking of biography, I have referred to novelists and historians, and used the work of poets, more than is usual in a lecture on the biographer's craft, it is because I would like to see a healing of that rift that opened up in the 19th century between history and literature—a rift from which biography, as the younger and perhaps illegitimate brother of history, has suffered greatly. It is a rift that has caused much clan warfare within the family of literature and led to a downgrading of literature itself in Western society. I believe that a cross-fertilization of ideas between fiction and non-fiction is vital for literature. Otherwise it becomes a plaything for specialists and crossword-puzzling scholars only: a game of Hunt the Symbol. The novelist is free to leave the world of facts and take a short cut to the truth through invention. The biographer hopes to achieve a similar end by the shaping of his facts; he is, in Desmond MacCarthy's famous phrase, "an artist on oath."

I see the position of biography in much the same way as Philip Guedalla saw it. He wrote that "biography is a very definite region bounded on the north by history, on the south by fiction, on the east by obituary, and on the west by tedium." It moves west, I would add, the more it is shunned by novelists, historians and the living reader: and the more it prides itself on being separate from them.

But history too suffers in isolation. Seen exclusively from the biographer's point of view, historians are like deaf people who go on answering questions that no one has asked them. That was Tolstoy's opinion. And it was in something of the same vein that Hegel decided: "All history teaches us that history teaches us nothing." You can see some verification of this, I think, in the historian H. A. L. Fisher's view of history as one emergency after another without pattern or premeditation. Or you can see it in A. J. P. Taylor's wry recommendation to statesmen to avoid the study of history from which they would most likely learn from the mistakes of the past how to make the same mistakes in the future. If history, as C. V. Wedgwood has suggested, gives the overall view of what happened, biography gives the eye-level view: and it is essential to combine these views in the multi-faceted view of literature.

This belief has been strengthened in me by a book I have recently been co-editing with Robert Skidelsky called *God's Fifth Column* by the late William Gerhardie. I would therefore like to end my lecture with some comments about this unusual work. Robert Skidelsky is of course a distinguished historian; I am chiefly a biographer; and William Gerhardie is best remembered as a novelist—the author of such novels as *Futility* and *The Polyglots* that excited tremendous acclaim from Evelyn Waugh, Graham Greene, C. P. Snow, Edith Wharton, H. G. Wells and others in the 1920s and 1930s. But his posthumous book is a work of non-fiction in which I hope the disciplines of history, biography and the novel have been combined. In his subtitle, Gerhardie calls it "a biography of the age." In fact it covers the years 1890 to 1940 through which he himself had lived. Part of the interest of the book, in this present context, lies in its criticism of pre-1940 historians and in the attempt Gerhardie makes, through imaginative literary devices, to improve on their methods. By that time the partial reformation of historical writing by historians such as E. P. Thompson had not taken place. There was less social history and more history of political power—the record of which had been "elevated" (in the words of Sir Karl Popper) "into the history of the world." In such records we may principally see an endless repetition of the wrong way of living. I can think of no better succinct example of what Gerhardie objected to among statesmen and historians than the words with which Winston Churchill celebrated the unconditional surrender of Germany in 1945. "A splendid moment in our great history," Churchill declared, "and in our small lives." This belittling of the individual, or what Gerhardie termed "the suffering unit," was a symptom of, almost an excuse for, our inhumanity to fellow creatures for which the conventional historian was partly to blame. "History will absolve me" announced Fidel Castro after his unsuccessful assault on the Moncada Barracks in 1953. By which he meant that there would be a procession of obsequious historians preening themselves on being asked to place their signature on such endorsements. To Gerhardie such an historian was "like a butler absorbed by his duty of rating the events he announces in the order of their conventional importance while keeping his private thoughts . . . to himself [and] too busy ushering in his facts, too replete with his ceremonious virtue [to] dwell on the disparity between their conventional and their human values."

By contrast, the artist-historian (which Gerhardie himself set out to be in this ambitious work) is, as it were, God's butler, and his business is to present a history that is by implication morally as well as factually accurate. If the old-fashioned historian had looked back only to the front pages of old newspapers to report the doings of politicians, Gerhardie opens the paper up to report on other aspects of life. His history is still peopled with men of action, but it also includes men of imagination such as Chekhov, Proust, Tolstoy—who do not usually appear in historical panoramas. Gerhardie depicts most politicians as being one-eyed people who see things clearly, but oversimplify in order to act. The men of imagination, seeing with both eyes open, have a truer perspective on life. His book takes the form of plotting one view against the other.

The term fifth columnist, originating in the Spanish Civil War, is perhaps less well-known than it was in 1939 when Gerhardie began this book. Four rebel columns were advancing in 1936 on Madrid under the command of General Mola who boasted in a broadcast that the soldiers of his four columns would be welcomed by their friends already waiting for them in the capital. These mysterious friends were soon being humorously referred to by the republicans as the fifth column. Gerhardie takes this idea and makes of it a philosophical concept to account for the motive power behind the march of history. Faith, hope, charity and mercy are the four columns in God's army: the fifth is divine discontent. It is the eternal corrective: comedy in a self-important age; tragedy in trivial times; and in a materialistic society, spirit itself within the gate of matter. It exists in all of us, particularly as that part of the truth we do not know or do not tell. It is behind our elevation into a national hero of a man such as Hitler: it lies in our failure to redeem our past history. We do not have to look far in our own times to see its workings.

Gerhardie disliked interpreting the events of his age by means of mechanical causes and effects—methods that turned the historian into a sorcerer's apprentice. But inevitably he has some mechanical explanations. Nationalism and usury (the latter defined as "the will at once to spend your money and keep it") he sees as the two main animators of destructive terrestrial projects. He propounds, too, various schemes for practical reform: abolition of sovereign states leading to a world federation, and a minimum guaranteed income for all to be levied from the profits (or what he termed "superflux") of industry. Here is an accurate reflection of the hopes and beliefs of the 1940s against which the achievements of the 1980s may be set in ironic counterpoint.

To that extent the book is a representative work; but in other ways, not least in the passion and the poetry of its argument, the artist's vision and the writer's use of language, it asks to be taken as an exceptional work. "The world of politics," Gerhardie wrote, "awaits its Proust." Norman MacKenzie, had he been with us, might well have argued that Beatrice Webb, in the forthcoming edition of her diaries, achieved this role. To what extent Gerhardie himself did so must be judged by critics and by the individual readers. In the meantime the significance of Gerhardie's book for contemporary biographers is that it may stand as a remarkable attempt, through synthesizing the skills of the fiction and non-fiction writer, to heal the division between history and literature. Looked at as such, I think it points to a more promising future for all of us.

Problems of Writing a Biography of a Communist Leader

PHYLLIS AUTY

Biographers of communist leaders are convinced that they have a more difficult task than that of any other writers. The non-communist western author who is not a Marxist is faced with the normal difficulties of biographers plus the problems of working in a foreign culture, associated with an alien ideology, and immense, sometimes insurmountable, obstacles in obtaining adequate and reliable sources. He is also faced with gigantic and all-pervading myths encrusting communist leaders; these prove almost impossible to test against historical truth because neither the subject, nor his (and so far they are all men) associates wish the truth to be made public. In spite of this, some biographers find the challenge of writing the life of an outstanding communist leader irresistible. Harold Nicolson believed that a biographer should not select a subject "outside the area of his general knowledge;" that he should be "as cautious in the choice of his subject as in the method he pursues." Biographers of communist leaders have to contravene both these rules. So great is the competition today to find a good subject for biography that caution goes to the winds, and unlike the Grub street biographers of the past whom Joseph Addison denounced as "watching for the death of a great man like so many undertakers, on purpose to make a penny of him," we the contemporary biographers of the modern Grub street, write biographies of great men and women, and especially of well-known communists, before they are dead, in the (often unfulfilled) hope of making a penny out of them when they are still alive, and before the full story can be told. It is what is known (and used to be condemned) as pre-empting the market.

Another eminent writer who has commented on the work of biographers is Sir Lewis Namier, who suggested that biographers write biography instead of history (thereby suggesting that biography is not history) because they are afraid of what he called "the unbounded field" of history. He believed that biography allowed the author to do a superficial job in three fields—he could select from basic sources without scholarly collation, only those that suited his purpose; he could use bits of elementary psychology at will without need for close analysis; and he only needed to sketch an elementary historical background. All these accusations could be leveled equally at historians and perhaps also at Namier himself who excelled in the discovery of minute facts about micro-personalities whose lives, he believed, made the texture of history in the way that the life of one person, however important, did not.

In fact, biographers of communist leaders rarely have the opportunity to select extensively from original sources. They have to make use of all the material they can find. Dearth of sources, one of their major problems, forces them to utilise all other techniques of biography including psychology, elementary or otherwise, and to use historical background (as for instance in Edward Crankshaw's *Krushchev*) to make up for lack of specific material about the lives of their subjects. The account of a life, and description of the background into which it is integrated, is as much a form of history as the micro-biographies of Namier or the more fashionable contemporary stories of the poor and oppressed as typified in Emmanuel Leroy Ladurie's *Montaillou*. All, including biography, are different ways of looking at life *wie es eigentlich gewesen ist*, and they complement each other.

Why Write Biographies of Communist Leaders?

Biographies need no justification. "The proper study of mankind is man;" and no excuse is needed for writing the lives of famous communists. It is true that biographies of Lenin, Stalin, Krushchev, Mao or Tito—or indeed of Solzhenitsyn, Pasternak, Djilas, Andrić or any other well-known communist figure only give a particular view of the histories of their countries and times. But more than half the world's population live under communist rule, and it is interesting and perhaps instructive for us to learn about their leaders and literary figures—how they emerged from obscurity, what kind of men they were and how the leaders used their power. If such biographies need justification, it is in the challenge to explore this relatively unknown territory, to find out more about that half of the world where people live under a system whose ideology has been the most important political dynamic of the twentieth century, affecting not only the lives of people who live under it, but all our lives in the world today.

If we look at the great communist leaders of our time, they are not, with the exception of Tito, at first sight attractive personalities to write about. But do we have to like the subjects of our biographies? I believe that strong feelings of like and dislike are a disadvantage when starting on a biography, though it is true that such feelings, and especially admiration and devotion, have often provided the main motivation for biography. An example of this approach to a communist leader is *Red Star Over China* by Edgar Snow. Vladimir Dedijer's *Tito Speaks* and Velko Vinterhalter's *Tito* might also be considered in the hero-worshipping category. Too much admiration for the subject makes the resulting work, if not hagiography, at least something in the nature of an icon. Hatred and dislike are also likely to render the work nugatory as in Deutscher's life of *Stalin*. More important when starting a biography is the judgment, rational rather than emotional, that the person was in some way important, his life influential and his character, whether judged good or bad, was interesting and complex. It has been said that biographers tend to identify with their subject whilst writing. That has not been my experience; though I found that I became obsessed with the character of Tito when writing about him, and my thoughts became dominated by the problems of trying to unravel the complexities of his character and life.

Special Difficulties for Biographers of Communist Leaders

A major difficulty affecting all search for information about any communist leader is that there is always an accepted official version of his character and life-story. This is all pervasive and is backed by material provided by a state propaganda department. The official life has usually received such total coverage in newspaper articles, media programs, films and interviews that it has come to be the accepted version and is believed by most people except those who may know something different but dare not reveal it. The subject himself, as time goes by, may even come to believe the myth and forget the truth. The strongest proponents of the official version are usually the government officials and associates of the leader, for their positions of power and privilege are bound up with the myth of the leader. The biographer, therefore, has to cope with a blanket of secrecy surrounding his subject and a conspiracy of silence about anything except the official information about him.

Official life-stories of communist leaders all have certain points of similarity which sound almost like nineteenth-century fiction. All had a poor deprived childhood—poverty, squalor and hunger caused by an exploiting, capitalist society; they worked hard at school (Stalin and

Mao were rebels at school; Tito was not); all were ardent readers at a time when few of the poor could read, and this was the early sign of their ambition. They became activists in political work; Stalin and Tito became workers for a short time and all moved to communism as a means of bettering themselves and society. They were imprisoned by harsh capitalist regimes and eventually led their parties to success through revolution. It is probable that the general scenario of this story was true for most leaders, though Ronald Hingley and other Stalin biographers are doubtful about many of the details in the official version of Stalin's early life; the account of Tito's, though somewhat romanticized, seems in general to stand up to examination where it can be checked. Mao, also brought up in a backward agricultural society had a rather different early life, for his father was a fairly prosperous peasant, and his early difficulties according to his own account, came from his rebellion against his father. The revolutionary experiences of these three leaders were individual. Mao's road to revolution was through the famous Long March; Tito's through his leadership of the Partisans in the Second World War. Stalin made his way through unremitting hard work for the Bolsheviks and brilliant party in-fighting after the death of Lenin. All communist leaders had to engage in power struggles on their way to the top, but Stalin was by far the most ruthless. Some parts of these stories are included in the official biographies and there are numerous articles written about them, especially in the cases of Mao and Tito, giving colourful anecdotes. The material is abundant; but when it comes to trying to check the stories against other evidence, the writer encounters heavy official obstruction.

Sources

Original source material about the lives of communist leaders is not normally made available to foreign writers, so it is very difficult to compile independent accounts of their lives. As Ronald Hingley pointed out in his *Life of Stalin*, his biographers are faced with a virtual absence of archival material, although he had reason to believe that an archive relating to Stalin's life did exist. Isaac Deutscher, biographer of Lenin, Stalin and Trotsky wrote "Clio, the Muse of History has failed to obtain admittance to the Kremlin." By Clio, Deutscher meant himself, as other biographers, more acceptable to the Soviet authorities, have been permitted to enter the Kremlin (notably some American scholars as well as Montgomery Hyde), but this has not greatly advanced their knowledge. It is assumed by students of contemporary China that there is an archive relating to Mao's life; but it does not appear to have been seen by any of his many biographers, who rely heavily on Mao's accounts of his own life—to Edgar Snow in the thirties and in 1971, on his *Collected Works* (up-dated and revised to correspond with later events) as well as on selections of his talks and speeches such as those edited by Stuart Schram in *Mao Tse-tung Unrehearsed* (1974). But all of these (with the possible exception of some material given to Snow) are predigested selected material which hinders as much as helps biographers. Neither in China nor in the Soviet Union is there the equivalent of the British Public Record Office or the USA archival deposits where scholars may work freely. It is known that the Soviet Union has rich archival holdings, but only occassionally and in an arbitrary way have any western scholars been allowed access and even then what is seen is strictly controlled. I know one scholar who worked on Soviet archives only to find that all proper names and dates had been carefully excised with a razor from all documents, which looked like perforated computer cards to the total confusion of researchers.

This is not to say that the Soviet Union and other communist countries are the only places where archives are tampered with or made available on a selective basis. Many writers have difficulty in obtaining access to archives in certain countries of western Europe including both France and Italy; and anyone who has worked on the Second World War in the British Public Record Office knows the problems of the critical gaps in certain sets of documents relating to people or events of particular importance. There are also problems connected with many private archives, including the Royal Archives at Windsor (UK) where the British royal family keeps strict control over what material is published about members of the royal family including material going back some two hundred years. In addition, all countries refuse to release their secret service papers, and this may be considered natural, but the problem with communist countries is that the areas that are categorized as secret are much wider than in most other countries and they consider any material, however mundane, as a matter for security.

This security surrounding communist archives also operates to control any privately held papers which may relate to the leader. Because of dire penalties against those who disclose unofficial material (see for example the sad fate of Stalin's aunt cited below), people who have been associated with communist leaders have been unwilling to admit that they have kept documents of historical interest, and many years may go by before this information can be disclosed. How much still remains hidden—in Russia, China, Yugoslavia, Bulgaria and other countries—it is impossible to guess, and the fear is that much knowledge about people and events will never be revealed.

However, material is disclosed from time to time that does not have the official stamp. This was the case with V. Mićunović's *Moscow Diary* (1980) published freely in Yugoslavia (in spite of Soviet protests). There is also the case of the mysterious publication in the USA of *Krushchev Remembers* (1972) about which to this day a puzzle remains as to how it was smuggled abroad, how far it is genuine and how much was concocted independently of Krushchev. There are also the numerous memoires published in the West by refugees from the Soviet Union and other communist countries. These are often inspired by great hatred of the communist regime under which the author suffered. They pose a special problem for the biographer who has to assess what is scientific evidence, what is fraudulent, and how much is distortion.

Material provided by the supporter of a communist ruler who then turns against the system is particularly difficult to assess. An example of this is to be found in the later works of the Yugoslav Milovan Djilas, formerly fanatical communist colleague of Tito, at one time tipped as his successor. After a dramatic change of heart, he became violently opposed to communism and was eventually imprisoned for publishing these views outside Yugoslavia. Today, he still lives in Belgrade and publishes abroad his memoires of the Tito period. These include a recent *Kritisches Biographie von Tito* (1980) with a little new unofficial material and some quite outspoken, critical, and malicious assessments of Tito from Djilas's standpoint. This kind of work, like other source material, needs to be used with caution and psychological understanding of the author's character and position.

The secrecy that applies to private memoirs and papers also proves an impediment when it comes to interviewing private individuals. Friends, relatives, colleagues and others can be interviewed by biographers trying to flesh-out the official life story, but unless those interviewed live outside the communist country (and sometimes even then), they are frightened to tell what they know about the leader. Stalin's daughter only gave an account of life with Stalin (*The Alliluyev Memoirs*, 1968) after she had escaped from the Soviet Union; Stalin's aunt who published innocuous memoirs during his lifetime, and probably with his agreement, paid the penalty of harsh imprisonment. In Yugoslavia even Tito's relatives and friends have so far proved unwilling to divulge information about his private or even about his early life; his enemies are even more discreet. There are plenty of accounts of Mao, but few that are personal and private, and though his wife Jiang Qing might be all too willing to talk, she seems unlikely in present circumstances to have the opportunity to do so, and might be highly unreliable if she did.

The biggest gap in source material on communist leaders is the almost total lack of their own private papers—no shoe boxes of love letters and bills. Letters from and to other people on private matters are the richest mine of information for biographies of literary and other personalities, and often also of non-communist political leaders, but these are not available for communist heads of state. They have been public figures so dedicated to political life that from an early stage in their careers their written records, however personal, had political significance and have been subject to control either by themselves or by their associates. Many must have been destroyed. Of course these leaders had private lives, and we know a little bit about their loves, friendships and family relationships; but I know of no abundant—or even sparse—collection of private papers from which a private biographer of a communist leader could work—nothing like the collections that exist for Roosevelt or Churchill, and certainly nothing like the papers that Michael Holroyd had for Lytton Strachey or George Bernard Shaw. It is a crucial loss which deprives communists' biographers of material for that progressive build-up of revealing detail in human exchanges which allows a writer to penetrate more deeply into the character he is studying; it also deprives the author of that telling evidence of character and experience by which the subject reveals himself. From the moment he becomes leader, if not before, the communist is at pains *not* to reveal himself. This is carried far beyond the normal mechanisms that ordinary people use to protect themselves from self-revelation. The motive in both cases is to conceal the truth; in the case of communist leaders the motive is strengthened by fear because both state and ideology are involved with the fate of the individual. Such secrecy results in a loss of historical material which is irreparable.

Printed Sources

When it comes to printed sources, the problem is not scarcity but superabundance. As soon as the communist leader's career is a matter of public record it is closely controlled by officials who decide what is suitable for publication. In the case of Stalin, this stage was reached soon after the death of Lenin and certainly from 1929; Mao's public record may be said to date from 1936 when he reached the Yenang base; Tito's public record dates from the time when he was recognised by the western allies in 1943; for Tito, like Mao, spent his formative years of leadership isolated from the outside world, and this to some extent might be said of Stalin before 1929. By the time these leaders attained supreme power, they were in control of their own propaganda machine which was used to promote their own leadership. Official appearances and speeches were recorded in their own and the world's press. Interviews were given selectively as is the case with other heads of state, but always the reporting and usually the interviews were strictly controlled. The purpose of all reporting was to reinforce the image of the leader that had already been decided on. These official records which the biographer must use to piece together the leader's lifestory cover acres of turgid prose. Foreign journalists, writers and even scholars have added secondary material, sometimes being themselves victims, willing or unwitting, of official propaganda. This was true in most of Stalin's interviews—those for instance by H. G. Wells, Emil Ludwig, Krishna Menon and perhaps also the Webbs and Bernard Shaw.

The Myth

Many biographers have to cope with the problem of how to deal with the myth which has taken over from the real person they wish to write about. Myths are also created around people who are not heads of state; political and literary figures and, in our own days pop-stars and athletic idols, all suffer this treatment. Though not new, this approach is one of the new directions of biographical techniques being much developed in our own times. Publishers and biographers are playing an increasing part in directing the creation of myths. There is, for example, the myth that was created around the figure of T. E. Lawrence after the first world war or that which was projected about Scott of the Antarctic. These myths have been debunked in our times by other biographers as were the Victorian myths that Lytton Strachey examined in *Eminent Victorians;* and one of the on-going directions of biography is the debunking of myths created by biographers or auto-biographers and the follow-up of biographies to examine the debunking.

In all cases of myth, I am inclined to think that the subjects themselves have been parties to, and actors in, their own legends. They do this as much for the purpose of creating a false image to replace the real person as for the purpose of self-glorification.

There have been cases of the auto-myth even nearer our own times. Perhaps this applies to Roosevelt and Kennedy as well as to Richard

Nixon who may have been less successful in his efforts. I might cite also the case of Lord Louis Mountbatten who had the distinction of preparing before his death, biographical material (posthumously shown in film on television), which was so preposterous as to destroy the noble myth of himself as great-leader-who-was-always-right that he had taken such care to try to create. Such myths are easier to debunk once the subject is dead; it is more difficult (and more dangerous because of libel laws) when the subject is living.

But the myth of the communist leader is different and more intractable. It may also be partly self-created, but it serves something more than self-glorification and self-justification. For much of this century the idea of the great heroic leader has been part of the power-structure of communist states, though it may be that this idea is becoming outmoded as we approach the end of the millennium. None of the successors of Stalin has been raised to the heights of myth that was concocted by and for him; this status was not allowed to Krushchev or Brezhnev, and the "cult of personality," as it was called when the great leaders became downgraded, is now denounced in the Soviet Union and in Red China. Perhaps such myths are abandoned when there is no one outstanding person ready to step into the leader's position.

There are many reasons why the myth of the great leader is important in communist states—partly because all the leaders who have been myths were associated with revolutions that were still young in historical terms and still struggling for acceptance in a hostile world. The idea of the perfect leader becomes a symbol of unity, a personification of ideals expressed in the accepted ideology and not present in the actual society. The leader is being used like a high priest to manipulate the masses. State control of all media is used to build up an image of a leader who must be followed unquestioningly. For this purpose, journalists and biographers, as well as all other people must be prevented from looking for the truth and exposing the myth. It may be that many people do not believe it, but state authorities go to great lengths to prevent their scepticism from spreading. So biographers, grappling with such myths, take on something much bigger than a normal scientific reinterpretation. Their search for truth is feared and opposed lest it undermine both the power of the state in question and the philosophical foundations on which that power is based.

This is well illustrated by the case of Stalin who controlled and supervised his own myth until shortly before his death. After his death, for a short time under Krushchev, there was an attempt to destroy the myth and substitute an anti-myth with material approximating more to the factual truth. This was begun by Krushchev in his famous secret speech to the Twentieth Congress of the Communist Party of the Soviet Union in which he gave details of the hecatombs of murders committed on Stalin's orders and of some of the false claims made in the creation of the Stalin-heroic-leader myth. This was followed by a considerable number of revelations about Stalin and his works which opened a revealing gap in the curtain of secrecy that had previously surrounded him. But this happy state of affairs did not last; it was found to be too damaging to the Soviet state both internally and externally, and this anti-myth was quickly suppressed to be substituted, not by the previous myth, but by almost total silence about Stalin's leadership. He became almost a non-person, but still a man about whom biographers were denied factual information.

The story of Mao has followed through similar and even more complex phases than that of Stalin. He was already a legend in China by the end of the Long March in 1936. It was after this that the myth of Mao the philosopher-leader began to be propagated in China through numerous articles—some giving stylized biographical material. The legend then received publicity in the west through Edgar Snow's biography based on Mao's own accounts of his life as given to the author and published in *The Autobiography of Mao Tse-tung as told to the writer* (1949). This account, published in English and subsequently translated into Chinese, remains to this day the basic biographical material about Mao. The material was the basis of Edgar Snow's *Red Star Over China* (1963) and it was expanded many years later after Snow went to see Mao again in 1971 and published (posthumously) in *China's Long Revolution* (1971). But before this book was published, the myth of Mao had already moved into the further phase of cult. He was almost deified as the personification of communist idealism and "invincible thought"—"the spiritual atom bomb" as he was called. Both Mao and his enemies in the party used the cult to rally support and unify the country. Today both legend and cult are being reappraised in China because of the current movement against the cultural revolution and the harm it did in China. The cult of Mao is being downgraded and it remains to be seen what new versions of the Mao myth are being prepared.

Perhaps the most grotesque example of communist cult leadership is that of Kim il Sung in North Korea, where the history of his emergence in 1946 as the nationalist/communist leader is so surrounded by structured mythology as to make a straightforward biography by outside writers extremely difficult because facts cannot be checked. Typical of available material for biographers of Kim il Sung is the *Short Biography* (1972) prepared by an official editorial committee with the purpose of lauding "the outstanding Marxist-Leninist and great revolutionary leader," the "great thinker, theoretician and revolutionary genius" who "in the half-century since (his birth) has travelled the thorniest path in modern history, fighting single-mindedly for the independence of the country and welfare of the people, the victory of the cause of socialism and communism and the triumph of the international communist movement and the anti-imperialistnational-liberation struggle." It is within this world of ideological commitment and manipulation of the record to fit a pre-conceived image that has become both myth and cult that the biographers of communist leaders have to work; and their efforts are fraught with outstanding, often insuperable, difficulties.

Tito: a Case-Study for Communist Leader's Biography

The case of Tito as a subject for a communist leader's biography is unique, but it still involves enough of the problems that are encountered in such biographies as to illustrate the general points made above. In the first place, Tito, as a personality, had more immediate appeal to a western biographer than any of the other leaders I have mentioned. No less a committed communist than the others, he was, unlike them, a European by birth and background and therefore more easily understood and interpreted by western biographers. Though his character was influenced by his sojourn in Tsarist Russia as a prisoner in the First World War and, later, in Soviet Russia as an employee and trainee of the Comintern in the Thirties, he still remained firmly a man steeped in the European tradition, understandable to western historians. This made him more understanding of the western world than any of his contemporary Russian or Chinese communist leaders. At the same time he had a profound understanding of Soviet politics and ways of thinking. These qualities, though modified by the defensive secrecy and suspicion that affected all who were trained in the Stalinist system, remained an essential part of his personality.

When he became leader in Yugoslavia he was more accessible to westerners, journalists and writers included. He gave many interviews to foreigners and had the self-confidence to talk on occasion, spontaneously about himself, about his ideas and about those parts of his life that he was prepared to make public. He gave interviews to biographers Sir Fitzroy Maclean, Konni Zilliacus, Sir William Deakin and myself from Great Britain and to a number of Americans including Cy

Sulzberger and Eleanor Roosevelt, to all of whom he spoke with considerable freedom. He also gave much autobiographical material to Vladimir Dedijer who published it in biographical form, and later for the same purpose he gave more information to Pero Damjanović and some to Velko Vinterhalter.

During the latter part of the Second World War (from 1943) he was in constant association with British and American officers. It was therefore possible for contemporary biographers to have plenty of secondary witnesses of Tito at work and to get their impressions of him as a man and leader. Thus the source material about Tito's life is abundant, but not equally so for all periods of his life. It is sparse for his childhood but not inadequate or untrustworthy as is the case with Stalin. The archives of the Austro-Hungarian Empire which provide birth registration, school and military service records are still available. For Tito also, police records of inter-war Yugoslavia are extant and where these cannot be obtained from Yugoslav authorities today, or where it may be suspected that they are only selectively available, they can be checked in German war-occupation archives which are accessible to scholars. These contain papers that German intelligence officers took from the Zagreb police files when they were trying to collect information about the leader of the Partisans whom they hoped to capture.

Archives relating to the Partisans in the Second World War are extremely numerous from Allied, German, Italian and Yugoslav sources. A great many of them, especially of the Partisan documents, have been published because Tito's regime was the first to get their war documents into print. Like all other countries the Yugoslavs have not made all documents or categories of documents available to scholars; and, as is almost always the case with other countries, those that are most interesting and relate to most delicate matters are the ones that are not available. This is a problem facing all biographers dealing with wartime history.

There are great gaps in documentary—and any other—evidence about the most crucial phases in Tito's life—episodes about which Tito himself has maintained silence and imposed it on others. On these matters, Tito seems to have decided on set answers that may not represent the whole truth. Such is the case about certain aspects of his life in gaol about which he gave highly romanticized accounts. This is also the case with the period between 1934 and 1941 when he was working for the Comintern and spent long periods in Moscow. For this period we have to rely on Tito's own brief and selective stories. His anecdotes, interesting and lively though they are, give only a very sketchy account of his work, contacts, political activities, private life, thoughts and feeling during these dangerous years of Stalin's terror and purge. Most of Tito's associates and colleagues at this time were imprisoned or killed. We do not know why and how Tito escaped a similar fate, though the reason may well be Tito's essential unimportance among foreign communists in Moscow in those years.

It is even difficult to piece together the dates of Tito's periods in Moscow and visits to Yugoslavia. Such dates seem innocuous enough and the record must be available somewhere, and presumably this is in the archive about Tito's life, the existence of which, when I was working on his biography, was kept secret. I managed to discover that it existed and where it was kept. I succeeded in getting permission to see it, but was only allowed to ask specific questions and receive brief answers. When I went a second time, with carefully prepared questions, I was told the archive did not exist and had never existed—although I had seen the card index and files. I did, however, have the opportunity to look at other valuable material containing copies of Tito's wartime exchanges of telegrams with Dimitrov, his boss in the Comintern, through whom he sent his almost daily reports to the Soviet leaders about Partisan activities, and these have mostly been published in Yugoslav collections. There is no doubt that one of the elements in the secrecy relating to Tito's life in the Soviet Union and to all his relations with Russian leaders is affected by Soviet insistence on secrecy in all matters affecting their regime. The Yugoslavs do not care to release what the Russians wish to keep secret for fear of impairing relations between the two countries.

The myth about Tito began as an early necessity in his political career, long before he was a world-renowned Yugoslav leader. It began after he left gaol in 1934 and became an underground worker in the illegal Yugoslav Communist Party. Always on the run from the police, travelling to Vienna and France, returning frequently to Yugoslavia, afraid of police spies and informers, he visited many places in Yugoslavia to set up local communist cells. He gave orders with the authority of the Comintern; was seen by other workers in the cause only briefly; and rarely revealed his identity. He was the Scarlet Pimpernel of pre-war Yugoslav communists. During the second world war, the legend of the illusive communist leader became more widespread. German and British intelligence services were for some time mystified about this unknown but successful leader of a guerrilla army. So little was known about him that many thought he was an infiltrated Russian—Draža Mihailović, leader of the Cetniks, probably believed this to the end.

But from 1943, the legend of Tito-heroic-national-liberation leader had taken root. It was based on established fact and undeniably dramatic events. He had created an army which—without outside help or recognition, and lacking arms, medicines and even adequate food—managed to escape repeated German attempts at encirclement and annihilation. The hero-Tito image was fostered by a crude but highly successful propaganda department of the Partisan army; articles, posters, speeches, songs, every possible means was utilized to create the Tito legend as a means of uniting Yugoslav people behind the Partisans. Tito lived up to the part and his movement was crowned with success. The legend became a myth which dominated the character and interpretation of Yugoslav history of the Partisan war down to our own times. In this myth, truth and legend are so inextricably intertwined as to baffle historians and biographers even today.

After the war, as head of state Tito continued to be portrayed in this legendary rôle. The myth was taught to new generations and was increased by new real-life exploits. In 1948 another dimension was added to the Tito myth when he quarreled with Stalin, asserted Yugoslavia's independence, defied the might of the Soviet Union—and won. Even the rest of his life was not an anti-climax as was shown by his funeral in 1980 in Belgrade. It was attended by monarchs and heads of state from all over the world, including the Soviet Union, and was comparable in pomp and magnificence with any funeral of a great leader in modern times.

The anti-climax came after his death and it is at this stage that the myth became cult, erecting yet another barrier between the biographer and historical truth. The posthumous idea of Tito was now as important to the regime as the myth had been during his lifetime. There were now additional reasons why biographical material could not be made freely available.

With Tito, the biographer is aware of a very real individual hiding inside the legend, but the problem is how to get at him. He is easier to find than other communist subjects, but I have yet to read a biography of any communist leader that is able to convey adequately the private, as well as the public, personality.

The official biography of Tito has now to be written as a pious duty; many editors will be arguing not only about what is true or false, but also about what is suitable to be published. Teams of research workers will be needed to make a compendium biography. And, indeed, the material about Tito's life during the war and that covering his 35 years of post-war leadership in Yugoslavia is so voluminous, even without the material that has not been divulged, that it would be very difficult for it to be handled by one writer. This is the classic dilemma of modern biographers. How can one person handle such a mass of material? Should the work be attempted by one individual undertaking many years of work—as for instance in the case of Churchill's biography begun by Randolph, his son, and now being written by Martin Gilbert? Or is a biography of a man with such a complex and full life better written by teams of experts—military specialists, political scientists, psychologists *etc*? Is such teamwork likely to produce a better biography (and "better" must be defined in terms of historical truth, character interpretation, readability and feeling for the real man) than that produced by one author giving his own interpretation of all these aspects of life? Can one person be as professional as a team? I leave the questions unanswered, but would add that in Tito's case, he rejected every draft for his own biography that was submitted by teams of researchers.

However much we prefer the individual biographer, there is the danger that modern technology (including now computerized records) has made it possible to record too much about important lives; that it is, in fact, impossible for one person to deal with all the material; and that aided or composite biographical writing will be in the future the only way to handle material. We are also faced with another type of biographical writing and that is the "hyped" biography of the person who makes headline news. This is the book-of-the-film type of biography, sensationalized to a pattern, advertized at great expense, and packaged for gigantic sales in drug stores and supermarkets. "Hyped" biographies are the results of new directions in publishing in which new sales techniques have superseded the literary and historical values prized by publishers in the past. We have to hope that all these different types of biography can continue to live side by side; that the bad will not drive out the good; that biographers will learn to cope with voluminous material and maintain the standards of traditional biographical writing so that biography in our day can come to be recognized as a discipline in its own right.

Group Biography:
Challenges and Methods

MARGOT PETERS

Group biography may be defined as the interweaving of a number of lives by one writer to show how they interact with each other. These lives may be linked in common by any number of forces: a family, a place, an organization, a movement, a cultural affinity, a point in time. But implicit in group biography will be the notion that the individual is less than the whole, that the sum is greater than any of its parts.

Group biography is arguably a modern biographical development. It would not have occurred to Plutarch, although he did contrast the Greek and Roman character; nor to those early biographers, the chroniclers of saints' lives. Samuel Butler, creating his Theophrastian "Characters" in the 17th century, saw that people are less individuals than types, but did not try to interlace his characters to show how one social type creates another. Samuel Johnson gathered the lives of the poets together between two covers, made some astute comparisons and contrasts (notably between Dryden and Pope), yet left each life as intact as if it had been bound separately. Nineteenth-century biographers of such eminent Victorians as Scott, Carlyle, Charlotte Brontë, or Dickens viewed their subjects as monolithic: they tower against the landscapes of Lockhart's, Froude's, Gaskell's, and Forster's lives.

Then came Darwin to tell the Victorians they were not fallen angels but risen apes; Marx and Engels to classify by economic class; the gradual collapse of Empire; a democratizing war; and, of course, Freud. W. H. Auden summed the latter's influence in the poem "In Memory of Sigmund Freud": "No wonder the ancient cultures of conceit," wrote Auden, "in his technique of unsettlement foresaw/ the fall of princes." In this new atmosphere of scepticism Lytton Strachey set out to topple four of these princes. He selected carefully: the churchman, the evangelical imperialist, the Christian educator, the first career woman—Victorians eminent not only for their wills to power, but for the hypocrisies they were forced to adopt to justify those wills. This common theme of the four lives, the brevity of the biographies, and Strachey's elegant malice which spares no weakness, whether it is Cardinal Manning's fondness for reviewing his four red folios or Florence Nightingale's encroaching senility, give *Eminent Victorians* unity and pose it as a candidate for group biography. Yet Strachey makes no attempt to connect the four otherwise: and indeed his characters are less noted for making connections with other individuals than for overpowering them.

Biography has not been the same since Darwin, Freud, and Strachey. Yet although we no longer have heroes, modern biography has grown to heroic proportions in the life writer's eagerness to examine and expose. We have become subjects for clinical description, exhaustive case studies, banks for data. Current practice dictates that even minor figures require two volumes: witness Yvonne Kapp's recent biography of Eleanor Marx which runs a daunting 1,160 pages, more than accorded to her father. We are afflicted with the *omnium gatherum* mentality that Richard Altick deplored. And, since truth is a relative quantity, a new biography of the same subject can be justified every other year.

Group biography offers a welcome antidote to the overdocumented tendencies of biography today. In one sense, of course, it may be the desperate biographer's last frontier. Pity the poor biographer interested, for example, in Henry James or Mark Twain. Quite impossible (one would say) to begin another life of either. But if one were to consider them along with Whistler, Crane and Pound as London Yankees, then new facets of the old subjects might be turned toward the light. Or pity the biographer interested in Bernard Shaw. Three hefty tomes by Shaw's authorized biographer Archibald Henderson behind, as well as numerous biographies by his contemporaries, and an authorized biography in several volumes ahead. But if one took only a narrow slice of Shaw's life—his association with the New Women who were acting the New Drama on little money and a great deal of faith—and explored the cross-currents of influence among Shaw and actresses such as Janet Achurch, Florence Farr, Marion Lea, and Elizabeth Robins, then new patterns might emerge, new aspects of Shaw and the actresses reveal themselves. In a very practical sense, therefore, group biography offers another shot at a subject whose life has already been well documented as individual, yet whose various relationships may not have been analyzed in depth.

Conversely, group biography allows a writer to recover the lives of persons who may not warrant separate volumes, but who may have led interesting lives even though they did not make it into the *D.N.B.* This is not so much true of the Bloomsbury group, nor certainly of Stanley Weintraub's *London Yankees;* it is true of the MacKenzies' *Fabians,* a group biography that allows us a look at such less well-known socialists as Edward and Marjorie Pease, Frank Podmore, and Graham Wallas. As for my own experiment with group biography, I have to admit that perennially important and provocative as Bernard Shaw is, the feminist actresses and managers who risked jeers, libel, unpopularity, and certain loss of income to put the New Drama on the stage were quite as interesting as the playwright whose great fame has all but obliterated them from the record. Shaw himself helped along the obliteration by deleting the names of Janet Achurch, her husband Charles Charrington, Elizabeth Robins, and Marion Lea from his revised version of *The Quintessence of Ibsenism.* In the first edition he had given them credit as the pioneers of the New Drama in London, the innovators who made his own drama palatable to audiences reluctant to be shocked and harrangued. His diary also testifies to the impact made upon him by the Ibsenites: the Charrington production of *A Doll's House* in 1889 was arguably the catalyst that made him realize the stage rather than the soap box could be his platform. His second play *The Philanderer* laughed at the New Drama; his fifth, *Candida,* written for Janet Achurch, turned Ibsen upside-down, showing that the doll in the house was the husband, not the wife. Meanwhile his *Quintessence* had made him the leader of the Ibsenites in London, while his first play was chiefly memorable for New Woman Blanche Sartoris throttling her maid. New Woman Florence Farr played Blanche, and in 1894 gave him his first success by commissioning and staging his *Arms and the Man* at the Avenue Theatre. There were two major social issues fermenting during Shaw's early years in London: the emancipation of the working classes and the emancipation of women. The emancipation of the working classes had little stage potential; the emancipation of women enormous. Shaw saw it, approved it, and used the movement to his own advantage. Reading the *Quintessence* today, we would believe that he and Ibsen were the pioneers of modern drama in England. Without in the least denying Shaw's genius, I have tried to show in my group biography that the founding of the New Drama was a composite effort, and that Shaw did not so much create the New Woman as use her.

But these explanations for group biography—that it allows new perspectives of both major and minor subjects—are comparatively superficial. I called the form a modern development of the art of biography.

And that is because the form reflects certain historical, sociological, and psychological assumptions about human nature that have only recently seeped so deeply into the bedrock of our thinking as to form a natural basis for the writing of lives. Carlyle's famous dictum "The History of the World is but the Biography of great men" became a Victorian platitude; but as the twentieth century wore on, it began to seem far more probable that great men were created by the accidental circumstances of history. Certainly Shaw's Nietzschean superman seemed unattractive to many British intellectuals, even while Hitler and Mussolini were fulfilling the prophecy on the Continent. Shaw's creation of the larger-than-life G.B.S. annoyed Bloomsbury: Virginia Woolf found the colossal ego childish and boring. What she was really expressing was a whole generation's rejection of the patriarchal superman: the Victorian giants whose unchecked wills had led civilization— or so it seemed—to the brink of destruction, the nineteenth-century romantics who aggrandized the self above all. This revolt shaped the modern novel. Gone were the triumphant progresses of Tom Jones, Pamela, Pip, and Jane Eyre over all obstacles; in modern fiction characters overlapped, impinged, shifted in subtle patterns of interaction, the fates of each depending less on the assertion of individual will than upon the success or failure to interpret a gesture, keep an appointment, understand the unspoken desire in another heart. While the goblin motif of Beethoven's Fifth Symphony stalks through E. M. Forster's novel *Howard's End* like the footfalls of coming Fascism, crying "Panic and emptiness, panic and emptiness," another motif asserts itself even more strongly—the motif Forster chose as the motto for his book: "Only connect." It might be the motto for much modern fiction, even while that fiction deplores the impossibility of connecting. It is, in many ways, a feminine sentiment, in opposition to Victorian male giantism: the view of culture as the biographies of great men. It is significant that Forster in his essay "What I Believe" declared his trust in love and friendship rather than in Great Men, and that the first modern biographer was the feminine Lytton Strachey who exposed, deflated, and trivialized the gigantic heroes who had dominated his childhood. Biography lags far behind fiction in form: perhaps it cannot imitate it. Yet group biography may be the belated development in biography that parallels the early twentieth-century development of the novel. It too could take for its motto Forster's "Only connect." It too sees that the course of human events depends less on individualism than upon the endless ramifications of human interaction, much of which is beyond control or even consciousness.

It is significant that so many group biographies have been written about the late Victorian and Edwardian periods, years that saw monolithic structures of church and state fracture into a thousand sects, associations, fellowships, coteries, clubs, sisterhoods, communes, collectives, federations, institutes, guilds, unions, councils, leagues, congresses, parties, schools, movements, circles, boards, committees, fraternities, and alliances. Truly, as Yeats would write, "Things fall apart; the centre cannot hold." The Pre-Raphaelites, the Rhymers Club, the Social Democratic Federation, the suffragists, the Ibsenites, Bloomsbury. Bloomsbury might call itself a house of lions, but compared to the roars of Victorian lions like Macaulay, Mill, Carlyle, Dickens, Darwin, George Eliot, and Marx these are treble voices, the chorus rather than the bass solo.

Communalism was replacing individualism. At the magnificent Lyceum Theatre in London in the late 80s and 90s, the great actor-manager Henry Irving was playing out the last act of his solo as Shakespearian superstar. He sensed a change in the air without being able to change the way he had always created the fabulous Lyceum spectacles. For Irving it was the single-star system: the great actor spotlight center, other parts cut, his own padded, he alone controlling direction, production, script, cast, tempo, mood. In the same decades, in matinees at shabby theatres, obscure actors were staging cooperative ventures in the New Drama that would revolutionize the theatre: dramas without hero or heroine, without limelight, without "supporting" cast. Their efforts coincided with those of Harley Granville Barker, Elizabeth Robins, and Marion Lea to rescue Shakespeare from the hands of Irving: to restore simple stage sets, minor parts, original lines, scenes, and acts—to rebalance the whole. Content, evidently, to fashion the colossal G.B.S., but reluctant to tolerate rivals, Bernard Shaw ruthlessly chopped away at Irving's superstar mentality in the *Saturday Review,* urging a municipal theatre, a state-funded drama. "In a true Republic of Arts," raged Shaw, "Sir Henry Irving would long ago have expiated his crimes against the drama on the scaffold." "The single-star system is dead," Shaw advised Mrs. Patrick Campbell, who wanted to hire a fourth-rate Higgins unable to compete with her Eliza Doolittle. He was right. Certainly Lena Ashwell, who created his Lina Szczepanowska in *Misalliance,* felt the committee atmosphere of Shaw's plays. "No actor can make a real impression in Shaw's plays," she complained. "No one can say that so and so was great in a Shaw character as one would say he was a great Shylock or Macbeth." Although we may not agree, Ashwell put her finger on the communal, the operatic quality of

Shavian drama which was, of course, a reflection of the communal spirit of the times. Mrs. Patrick Campbell, sweeping into the Court Theatre to play Hedda Gabler, found that, although she packed the house, she was taken off after a week. Barker was firm: the Court was a repertory theatre offering a balanced selection of plays with balanced casts. Stars like Mrs. Campbell and Ellen Terry were misfits in such a system: the New Drama was a group effort, a committee proposition. Certainly, like Bloomsbury or the Fabians, it was a subject readymade for group biography.

Political, sociological, and psychological theory has furthered this shift in perspective from individual to group. Maynard Keynes, for example, went from the classical atomized theory of laissez-faire capitalism to a system of large-scale governmental (group) planning and spending: the Western nations went with him. None of the social sciences consider the individual apart from the group. Reading Leon Edel's *A House of Lions,* I was tempted to draw sociograms: Lytton and Thoby, Maynard and Lytton, Lytton and Duncan, Duncan and Vanessa, Maynard and Duncan, Clive and Vanessa, Thoby and Clive and Vanessa and Virginia, Lytton and Vanessa and Leonard and Roger, Lytton and Roger and Duncan and. . . . After isolating the ego and superego, psychology has sought to de-isolate them again. One need mention only the moving of the patient from the psychiatrist's couch out into group therapy, family therapy, encounter groups, role-playing groups, T-groups, and assertiveness training groups.

Although I would thus suggest that group biography springs from a modern world-view, I would not like to suggest that biographers approach their groups the same way, or that group biography has a common form, although chronological time probably dominates most group biographies as it does life itself. Certainly it dominates Stanley Weintraub's accounts of a family in *Four Rossettis,* of T. E. Lawrence and Bernard Shaw in *Private Shaw and Public Shaw,* and of the London Yankees. A typical chapter of *London Yankees* begins, "Early on the morning of January 8, 1913, the tenant of the Bungalow, Reynolds Road . . ."; the march of time also dominates within chapters, such as the account of Stephen Crane, which begins with him coming to London, spending four days, sailing for Crete by April 8, in early June returning to London, producing well the second half of 1897, by December pleading for advances, in the spring of 1898 writing at the top and bottom of his form, then back to Cuba on August 12, 1898, and so forth. This strong time-marking overshadows the announced theme of place, London, a theme supported by place-name chapter heads such as Tedworth Square, Lancaster Gate, and Tite Street. London does not really create a group for these lives, which remain separate and externally delineated by days, months, and years. There is, of course, nothing wrong with chronological organization: most biographies have it. But it does make Weintraub's book less experimental as far as form goes than its title seems to promise—and, since form reflects content, perhaps less experimental in content as well.

Another biographer has been truer to his announced place motif, Bloomsbury. The first sentence of Leon Edel's group biography *A House of Lions* heralds its strong place sense: "If we seek the beginnings of our story, we might start in various parts of England or Scotland or Wales, or in Cambridge, where the Bloomsbury males were educated, or even in some ghetto of Europe. But we might as well start in Bloomsbury itself . . ." The nine characters are largely defined by the places they were born, grew up, matriculated. It is apparent, for example, that Leonard Woolf's Jewishness is enforced by middle-class Brighton and St. Paul's, "the environment of a middle-class intellectual and city-bred boy." Similarly, Clive Bell is defined by his Wiltshire hunting and fishing-manorial origins, the house filled with stuffed animals, the board groaning with game. And the lives of the Stephen girls, Vanessa and Virginia, are dominated by the haunted house at No. 22 Hyde Park Gate, even though they escape from it.

Place descriptions have more importance than descriptions of persons: Thoby's room at Cambridge with its round table, photograph of the student's mother, books, and wicker armchair; or No. 22 Hyde Park Gate, "a seven-story angular awkward pile of stucco and red brick." As the saga of Bloomsbury unfolds, its growth is traced from place to place: to No. 46 Gordon Square, where the four Stephen children went to live after Leslie's death, the drawing room of which, with its blue and white curtains, pianola, early Victorian table and basket chairs, "very quickly became the center, the heart of the Bloomsbury of our story." That heart, however, was forced to beat in a number of locations as the Bloomsbury nine changed partners again and again in their intricate dance. The next branch office was No. 29 Fitzroy Square, where Virginia Stephen set up housekeeping with her brother Adrian. It is not reading too much into place description to suggest that the blue and white and wicker of Gordon Square was appropriate to Bloomsbury at that time: new, chaste, wary—masculine and feminine egos experimenting cautiously with different methods of oneupmanship. By the time Virginia hangs red curtains in the green carpeted drawing room of No. 29 Fitzroy Square, however, the words "semen" and Virginia's favorite, "copulation," had been uttered; indeed, "Sex permeated our conversation," Virginia wrote: "the word 'bugger' was never far from our lips." By the Brunswick Square phase, Bloomsbury, in current psychobabble, was conspicuously laid back. Murals by Duncan Grant, nudes painted by Adrian on his cupboard doors, champagne in the mornings, parties, parties, parties: the cultured, leisured, bohemian setting had been created for an intelligentsia whose "place" to a great extent gave them the privilege of being avant-garde. In one sense, of course, Bloomsbury was not a place at all, but something abstract—a tone, an attitude, a resistance, a movement created by the contradictions and similarities of its members. And Edel's biography traces abstract patterns (the word occurs frequently) as they shift and re-group. Yet the biography is permeated by place. It is the starting place for Edel's story, and its ending: it is the book's unifying motif.

A very different group were the Fabians, subject of a 1977 biography by Norman and Jeanne MacKenzie. Chiefly heterosexual as opposed to the homosexual or androgynous Bloomsburians, comprised largely of the educated lower-middle and middle classes rather than a Cambridge elite, as diversely cultured as the Anglo-Irish "downstart" Shaw, the aristocratic Beatrice Potter, and Ramsay MacDonald, the illegitimate son of a Scots housekeeper and a ploughman—the heterogeneous Fabians pose an obvious problem for the biographer. Neither socially nor culturally can they be thought of as a group. Nor can place be a unifying factor, since Fabian policy was forged by Shaw scribbling in his notebook on underground trains and park benches, by the Webbs in the Surrey hills, and by H. G. Wells at Sandgate. Sheer numbers make the group difficult to control: in the first chapter alone the MacKenzies introduce more than 45 persons relevant to the Fabian Society's beginnings, from the famous (Marx, Ruskin, Gladstone) to the obscure (Clarke, Taylor, Jupp). Nor were the socialists united in their thinking, but were splintered into Social Democrats, Marxists, Christian Socialists, Anarchists, Simple Lifers, Land Reformers, and Ethical Socialists (to name a few); and the Fabians divided among these. When some Fabians did try communal living in a Bloomsbury establishment of their own, the result was not satisfactory. "Fellowship is Hell," pronounced one disillusioned individual.

How to approach this complex, disunified subject? Strict chronology was obviously a necessity, and the biographers guide us surely from the initiation of the Society at the home of Edward Pease on October 24, 1883 to the death of Pease in 1955, the last surviving Fabian. Another obvious necessity was to focus on key Fabians, the Junta comprised of the Webbs, Shaw, Sydney Olivier, Graham Wallas and, later, H. G. Wells. Here, however, the reader stumbles upon inconsistency. The MacKenzies' method is to provide a biographical background for each Fabian as he or she is introduced into the developing account of the Society. Supposedly each member of the Junta is of equal importance; yet Olivier gets a mere six paragraphs of introduction and Sidney Webb only four, while Shaw merits sixteen and Beatrice Webb forty. The bulk of the biographical material about both Beatrice and Shaw involves their love affairs—Beatrice's with Joseph Chamberlain and Sidney Webb, Shaw's with just about everybody. There is good reason, of course, to describe the courtship of Beatrice and Sidney Webb, since it was founded upon a philosophy that would profoundly influence their work in the Fabian: the belief that as partners they would serve the community more effectively than either acting alone. But this is not true of Shaw's philanderings; and their irrelevance becomes more evident when we find something as important as Shaw's contribution to the *Fabian Essays,* for example, rather lightly skipped over, while his affairs with Jenny Patterson, Alice Lockett *et al.* are detailed at considerable length. It seems a case of the material ruling the biographer, rather than the biographer ruling the material, one of the chief hazards of life writing, as all of us who attempt it know. Indeed, focus and proportion are particularly difficult to achieve in group biography with its complex of subjects; they present the key formal problems of this type.

I dare to comment only because, having written a group biography, *Bernard Shaw and the Actresses,* I have experienced myself the formal and contentual difficulties of managing a large cast of equally important characters in one biography. In a preface to *A House of Lions,* Edel remarks that in the midst of his James biography he dreamed of writing a simple series of portraits, having determined never again to undertake so huge a task as Henry James. In the midst of my Shaw biography, discovering that I had to know the entire life histories of all the women with whom Shaw was involved (no paltry number), I vowed I would never again undertake so huge a task as group biography. It was not only the sheer mass of material needed to write the book that was daunting; it was the formal plan, the management of the mass.

Unlike any of the biographies mentioned above, mine had a major character, Shaw himself. This built-in focus tempted me in early days to consider separate chapters: Shaw and Janet Achurch, Shaw and Florence Farr, Shaw and Elizabeth Robins. But for me the essence of biography is the unfolding of a story: I would have all biographies fol-

low the irresistible curve of *The Rise and Fall of Barry Lyndon.* I decided, therefore, to make the biography chronological, as though Shaw
and all the characters were actually living the story I was about to tell.
The chapter heads are all in years, and Shaw's story is pursued from
his arrival in London in 1876 to his death in 1950, although the bulk of
the narration concerns his years as a rising playwright, 1880–1910. But
the chronological organization, I believe, tells comparatively little
about the thick tissues of relationships that the story accreted as it
grew. And besides, although Shaw progressed chronologically, the actresses did not, since at each reappearance I felt it necessary to stop the
action and summarize what she had been doing since last in touch with
Shaw.

In this way, I found a pattern and a tempo emerging: Shaw steadily
marching forward; the women appearing alternately and often retro-
spectively and only in their connection with Shaw. This pattern began
to embody a theme, a theme I was not wholly aware of when I began.
Here was Shaw—confident, invincible, increasingly successful, buoy-
ant, richer and richer, seemingly more and more youthful the older he
got—and, in contrast, the actresses, who either did not succeed, like
Florence Farr; or gave up acting, like Elizabeth Robins; or ruined their
careers with drugs, like Janet Achurch; or were hopeless amateurs, like
Molly Tompkins; or were past their primes and begging Shaw for
roles, like Ellen Terry and Mrs. Patrick Campbell. From their histories emerged for me the theme that the creative life of an actress is a
short and ephemeral thing, since she is simply the vehicle for the word;
but that the life of the artist as the creator of the word is long. Shaw
knew this. He was conscious always of immortality: Mrs. Campbell
complained of his constant reminders that his part of their correspondence was destined for the British Museum; she knew she would go
down to posterity as a footnote to his life. But in broader terms, I found
that my biography was about the old theme: life is short, art is long.

The British critic Arnold Kettle once made the simple but profound
observation that good fiction has both *life* and *pattern.* Biography obviously has life; single-subject biography, moreover, has one kind of
built-in pattern—the progress of the protagonist from cradle to grave:
beginning, middle, end. But Kettle meant more by pattern than this;
and if biography has not been taken seriously as literature, it is because
it lacks the patterning of theme, symbol, and imagery characteristic of
fiction. Group biography presents a particular problem for the biographer because it does not necessarily have even the basic life-progress
form. The writer is challenged to impose some kind of pattern upon

his or her material, whether it is the rapid "back and forth" movement that Weintraub establishes in his account of Private Shaw and public Shaw, or the "life is short, art is long" theme I found molding my disparate materials, or the recurring theme of place which bonds Edel's "string of beads," as he calls his Bloomsbury portraits. As a sub-genre, group biography is comparatively in its infancy, I believe. It offers, however, great experimental potential both in content and pattern, and its practice promises to expand the scope of biography considerably.

Biography: The Black South African Connection

N. C. Manganyi

Is there a place for biography, for the study of lives, for life writing in the continuing flux of change in black literature and culture in Southern Africa? This question, I believe, must be asked since all indications are that biographical practice in the Western World is now coming into its own. There is ample evidence to indicate this emerging significance of life history writing. It should suffice if we should note that the existence of the journal *Biography* is one aspect of the evidence I am referring to. Another aspect of note is the attraction that biographical practice engenders for interdisciplinary scholarship. This list could be extended.

Initially at least, two kinds of statements are necessary in dealing with the question of biography and the black experience. Both are statements of a descriptive and historical kind. We need to begin with several assertions that identify and characterise biography under Western eyes. Having done that, we need to scan a wide canvas of continuity and change in black culture and literature in search of manifestations of the verbal arts that we lump together under the term literature.

Biography is essentially a Western phenomenon and creation. Its absence or underdevelopment in non-Western societies is well known. In the West, where it has flourished to the best advantage, it is known to have gone through various transformations in both its theory and execution. Only broad generalisations are possible here and it should suffice if we should point out that several tendencies are notable in the development of biographical themes. There was a time when biography could legitimately have qualified as an elitist genre in terms of its audience as well as its subject matter. It assumed the form of laudatory narrative as if its entire purpose was didactic—the projection of ideal types of human personality. "The biography of praise, the laudatory chronicle, was a pre-Renaissance idealisation of man under God's rule. The Renaissance, with its emphasis on man as individual ushered in its opposite. Part of this was the biography of denigration."[1] This post-Renaissance emphasis on the individuality of man was to be brought to new heights of social, spiritual and cultural significance with the emergence in the West of "psychological man."

Biographers know only too well how these developments in the history of ideas and the concomitant changes in the social structure and values in Western societies have affected the theory and practice of life writing. Psychology and Psychoanalysis infused a new enthusiasm into what was to a large extent a literary and later a historical *leisurely* pursuit of sorts. Indeed, modern biographical practice is still reeling under the impact of the enthusiasm of the 30s and the 40s as well as the subsequent disappointments attendant upon the early promise of life writing. The increasing corpus of biographical theory is constantly receiving infusions from psychology, psychoanalysis, historiography (the new history), non-formalist literary criticism, and whether we like it or not from psychohistory. The practical response to this expanding theory is a decided concern with methodological problems in the execution of biographical studies, innovative attempts at multidisciplinary work as well as the emerging trend towards multiple biographies.[2]

Certainly this is a bird's-eye view of the state of biography in the Western World today. However, I believe this summary substantive enough to lead us to the next set of relevant observations. One conclusion which we can draw without any hesitation is that the prospects for biography in any society are related to structural and institutional forces that define and sustain a culture. More boldly stated, the biography of biography in the Western World is most decidedly related to the intellectual, cultural and technological history of the West.

Although such a statement normally requires substantiation, I will limit myself in this paper to highlighting relationships as I see them. I suggest the following linkages without developing them in detail. First, biography (including autobiography) developed as a literary genre. Its prospects in any society depend on the overall viability and level of development of its written literature. It is a narrative medium that is often equal in its scope to the novel.

Almost always, biographical writing is historical writing. Here then is another important condition for the flourishing of biography. A culturally institutionalised awareness and interest in the past, both individual and collective, is essential for the emergence and survival of biography. Needless to say, literacy is one of the major preconditions for a systematic historicity.

By the beginning of the present century, the consciousness of man in the Western World achieves higher levels of individualisation. James Joyce certainly brought this individualised consciousness to its apex with his stream of consciousness technique. Freud likewise was doing the same for individualised self-exploration in the technique of free association. In the "Waste Land" that Joyce, Freud and T. S. Eliot were responding to and constituting into an understandable arena Western man was retreating increasingly from community into a highly personalised consciousness. This development must surely be seen in the total context of the atomisation, alienation and anonymity that has come to be a singular feature of life in the large urban centres of the world. At the level of understanding, Darwin conquered nature and some of its mysteries for us and it remained for psychoanalysis and a depth literature (such as biography) to capture man's interior—his subjectivity. Man could move inward into the depths of his being.

In the historical dialectic that we are now considering, the literature of the West created a readership as the masses of men and women made new claims on literature to respond to the new human landscape that was evolving. Indeed biography in the West has emerged as one of the investigative narrative techniques *for the search of the new truth—the search for the inner truth of the subject.* This then is the state of biography under Western eyes. If we examine the history of biography in the West, we are likely to understand the prospects for its development in Africa. In Southern Africa we encounter a scenario that is different from the one I have just described in important respects.

Although the differences I am referring to are difficult to capture in a few statements, the next stage of my discussion requires that this be done in as parsimonious a fashion as possible. In spite of a possibility of a high degree of generalisability of the statements to be made for Africa as a whole, wisdom dictates that I limit my observations to South Africa and the BLS "archipelago" (Botswana, Lesotho, Swaziland).

In Southern Africa, we have a confluence of two major cultural streams. The Euro-Africans have sustained a dominant Euro-centric cultural stream since the earliest stages of interracial contact. On the other hand, Africans and other black groups have struggled in the face of psychological and physical subversion to maintain a majority culture whose hallmark is poverty and impotence in terms of power and institutional authority. The political dimensions of race conflict in Southern Africa are relatively well known. What requires explicit articulation in this paper are the prospects for life history writing.

I depend to a limited extent for this section of my paper on an earlier paper read recently at the University of the Witwatersrand Special Senate Lectures.[3]

I take as a starting point a statement by Mashangu, the main character in my piece entitled *Mashangu's Reverie*.[4] The following is what Mashangu (a black man) says to his white psychiatrist:

> I . . . I was thinking of repudiation. You know what I mean? I was looking at my life since the days at the Mission School. It has been one big battle repudiating, negating something or other—myself, my culture, even my people. You see, we're forced to speak only English on certain days at school. Mind you, not only to enable us to read Milton or Shakespeare at a later stage but to repudiate everything which was native to us. Can you visualise that? . . . Each one of us carries a double . . . a kind of replica of self that is always in conflict with the mask that faces the world. To protect this mask from its double, one cherished an illusion and nourished it—the illusion that the future and prosperity of the mask depends upon a negation of the past both individual and collective . . . .

What a colossal seduction into mindlessness! In the vocabulary of the urban black folk particularly in the 1930s and 40s is a little word: *Marabi*. It has taken on different connotations over time including a kind of African dance, a marathon "nice time" party, and just simply "good times." The South African writer Modikwe Dikobe developed this word and its meanings into a sustained metaphor in his novel *The Marabi Dance*.[5]

In the Marabi dance and the African ghetto music of the thirties and forties we witness a curious mixture of despair and tenacity. Something dies, is reborn and transformed. The African Marabi dance is the death and life cycle. It is, in my terminology, another social biographical statement on continuity and change in African culture. Ours has been a kind of cultural improvisation and like the Marabi dance our cultural progress has been open-ended. We have thrived in the midst of opportunity, cultural genocide and challenge.

In writing about cultural continuity and change in the African context one is entitled to use biblical images and say that indeed in the beginning of the cultural interface between the blacks and the whites *was the word*. Cultural genocide for us arose out of this supremacy of the word and the substitution of the vocal but unseen word (the oral tradition) for the word as a permanent symbol with a character all its own.

In time, the oral tradition with its preference for the dramatic moment and audience participation gave way to written literature with its individualising tendencies.

The oral tradition in African culture was at the time of colonisation epic and heroic.[6] Students of African Literature still need to examine this period to determine the extent to which the heroic oral poetry of the time was in some instances, if not always, some kind of biographical statement. Is it not true that praise, honour, idealisation and a historical sense were the defining elements in the traditional poet's performance matrix? For the moment, we should be content merely to take note of this fact and proceed.

Through more than two hundred years of cross-cultural transactions the oral tradition and its literature were subverted and subdued. Initially at least, the written word seduced us through promise—Utopia in the hereafter. The word of the missionaries was eschatological in its message and promise. Following the missionary effort and much later, after the South African wars of resistance, there was a significant transformation of the written word. Ideology in the form of popular scientific racism was tagged onto the theological and evangelical heroics of the early missionaries. Our literature did not, as we know more clearly today, disappear as a response to conquest. Conquest ushered in a movement towards a written literature which now exists side by side with our traditional literature. Towards the close of the last century and the beginning of the present one, black writers were beginning to respond to the stresses and strains of continuity and change in African culture and life.[7]

Needless to say, there is a sense in which written African literature in its infancy became a literature of capitulation. In its thrust for the cultural creation of the "New African" it leaned on the images that were projected by the salvation eschatology of the Missionaries and the robust but crude scientific racism of the times. Our brothers failed to see that the New African was a non-starter—that the New African was a cultural still-birth. This image was a conscious creation of the coloniser and not as is commonly believed, Narcissus in the face of the mirror marvelling at his own glittering reflection.

A work of art is a product of both culture and personality. Culture affects writers in various ways and writers when they are equal to the task impact on culture. What is involved in the relationship between writers and society is a continuing symbiotic thrust of influences and counter-influences. How refreshing it is to think, as I do, that a writer is a manipulator of images and of language. He is, indeed, the myth creator *par excellence.*

Recently, the South African writer Richard Rive provided us with an overview of imaginative writings by black South Africans writing in English.[8] I refer briefly to his assessment to complete my own brief historical review of black culture and literature. Rive's view is that three major phases in the development of black literature are discernable. We can identify an early period up to and including the Second World War. This early phase is followed by "protest writing" among members of "the Drum School" (1942–1970) and the "Soweto School" (1971–1973). The last phase, the contemporary phase, consists of writing strongly anchored in the black consciousness movement, a group that Rive describes as the "Staffrider School."

Naturally these distinctions are too neat and leave one with some degree of discomfort. Yet they are sufficient to suggest the major landmarks in the development of black writing in South Africa to enable us to locate the place of biography in this development of a literary tradition. During the early phase there emerged a tentative attempt at using the novel as a medium.[9] This was followed during the post-war years by the emergence of the short story as the medium of choice supported by the emergence of *Drum* Magazine in Johannesburg and the Harlem Renaissance in the United States.[10] The end of the fifties and the beginning of the sixties brought in a spate of autobiographies written almost exclusively by black South African writers in exile.[11] During the sixties exiled South African writers whose works were banned in South Africa experimented with various genres including criticism and poetry.

On the home front a literary revival dawned at the beginning of the seventies and this time the genre chosen was the poem.[12] In the seventies the predominance of the poetic mode is assured and yet the short story has also continued to hold its own.

Since this is not a paper on South African black literature, the outline provided is sufficient for purposes of creating a context from which we can isolate the prospects for life history writing. In this regard it is significant to note that in the 1930s an attempt was made to write very brief biographies of the elite.[13] This historically significant attempt did not, however, anticipate the emergence of biography as a literary genre amongst the blacks. It was part and parcel of the attempt at creating the New African that I referred to earlier in this paper.

From the point of view of biography practice and theory it is noteworthy that this genre has failed to thrive in the specifically black literary context. Various reasons have been advanced and continue to be advanced for the black writer's preference for short stories, and more lately poetry.[14] Since our main concern centres around the prospects for biography, we need not concern ourselves with these explanations at this moment.

Autobiography is a good starting point. Here the picture as we have seen already is one in which there was a quick upsurge in autobiographical writing precisely at that point in South African history when most of our black writers found themselves in exile in Africa, Europe and the United States. This occurrence certainly raises some crucial but complex questions, first about the operative socio-cultural and personality-related variables that sustain the creative impulse for autobiography. Second, the South African connection—our output in the realm of the autobiographical—suggests that the relationship between autobiographical writing and the writing of fiction is not a simple one. Explanations offered by the writers of autobiography themselves for choosing the autobiographical medium are often so simple and straightforward as to be totally unconvincing to a psychologist.

I would argue that an adequate accounting for the phenomenon we are now considering be sought in the interaction between an individual and the social, political and cultural influences that are brought to bear on him. The black autobiographer of the fifties (Mphahlele, Abrahams) and the early sixties (Hutchinson, Matshikiza, Modisane) seems to be saying a number of things. First, like all writers of autobiography, he believes himself to be someone who has something to say about his life. His life is singular like that of many of his contemporaries. He introspects and personalises experience in order to capture the vicissitudes of the lives of people in his community. Certainly in the case of those writers forced into exile, the autobiography is the most appropriate model for stock taking. Autobiography fortifies and sustains a shaky personal identity. It is one of these genres that enables individuals to use the past, to appropriate it (to "freeze the past" as one autobiographer put it), to own it in the hesitant attempts at forward movement. Autobiography in spite of its structure never has that quality of closure —of completeness. It is, for writers in exile, a kind of beginning in that the appropriation of the past is in the interest of self renewal and rejuvenation.

Significantly, the end of the fifties in South African black life signalled the end of the first literary renaissance. Black nationalism received at about that time one of the most lethal blows that Pretoria could bring to bear on political activity amongst the blacks. Indeed, those of our writers in exile who were writing autobiographies were doing so not only because there was a personal past to be celebrated but also because there was a communal black past that was sliding quickly into oblivion.

The autobiographies written by black South Africans that I referred to are part of an evolving tradition. It seems reasonable to hope that autobiography will always have an important place in our literary experiments. Its future is assured.[15] Quite clearly, when the black writer writes autobiography it will centre around his own life. Yet this life will intrigue us not only in terms of the ups and downs recounted, nor the subtleties of personality but in terms of *how this "autobiography" is a biography of the people.* What about biography proper?

For myself, I make bold to say that biography and the novel must be coupled together like fraternal (not identical) twins when one considers the sociology and history of any national literature. Both require an imaginative mastery of narrative technique as well as a flair for characterisation. As panoramas of created and recreated life, their scope is often of the same dimension. This is most certainly not literature for the ordinary working class man and woman. Both the novel and biography require a serious investment of time both at conception and at the level of the readership. These features of both the novel and serious biography determine in large measure their prospects in developing communities such as those that exist in the Third World.

As for us in South Africa—the black South African connection—sustained imaginative writing (fiction) has not up till now been our main forte. We do not have a strong tradition to lean on. As a working class majority, we are not surprised by this reluctance of the imagination to thrive in the direction of jumbo novels and equally unwieldy biographies. We are aware of an undeclared moratorium on biography until such time as the South African political situation provides for a greater climate of freedom and the dignity of individuals. The search for the new truth which is the hallmark of biography, however defined, is the product (as I have tried to show above) of freedom, respect for the individuality of persons. Our major struggle is still out there in the social environment and the journey inwards is still tentative.

Yet, ironically, certain varieties of biography would do a great deal to preserve our history and create a new heroism. I see multiple biographies and biographies in the psychohistorical mode as varieties best suited for vitalising the black South African connection in the telling of lives.

In situations in which oral history is more alive than written history, the study of lives in the spirit of the sociological imagination may yet reward us with a more authentic appreciation of the history of captive societies. Needless to say, in Africa and much of the Third World the romantic preoccupation with selfhood, which is a distinct creation of "psychological man," is only beginning to manifest itself. Yet here too, psychobiography, by focusing on the individual and his social and historical world, may broaden and sharpen our historical perspective. The study of lives in their social and historical contexts must surely be more germane to the study of life in historically extreme situations.

Naturally, no one in the world is entitled to claim a monopoly of agony, suffering and dehumanisation. Yet, it is probably true to say that metaphysical anguish is tolerable compared to the degradation of the "wretched" of the earth who are condemned to live without a meaningful past in order that they may forfeit the present and the future. Indeed, to be oppressed, subjugated, is to be forced to live without a past. In the history of individuals and societies, the *appropriation* of the past serves a restitutive function, and there is no doubt that in the social and cultural spheres, blacks in Southern Africa can only benefit from such an appropriation of the past as biography makes possible. I am suggesting that in politically extreme situations, such as we have in Southern Africa, the value of biographical studies has to be something more than cultural play, myth-creation and literary adventure. Biography in particular must uncover for us the meaning of Africanhood as an immutable reality in the specific and special circumstances of the historical saga of the subcontinent. Blacks in Southern Africa are people whose history has been put in cold storage—silent. The thrust of white power has ensured that the history-making voice of blacks is kept silent through imprisonment, bannings and in some cases forced exile. It is this silence that needs to be disturbed—this muted consciousness which can be appropriated and made manifest, vocal and articulate through the study of lives. Biography in this context cannot be preoccupied only with the vicissitudes of the individual self. It *must* concern itself with the individual and the historical moment. Indeed: "The life of an individual cannot be adequately understood without references to the institutions within which his biography is enacted"; and indeed also, "neither the life of an individual nor the history of a society can be understood without understanding both."[16]

NOTES

1. Robert Gittings, *The Nature of Biography* (London: Heinemann, 1978), pp. 21–22.

2. Noel Manganyi, "Psychobiography and the Truth of the Subject" (Unpublished ms.).

3. Noel Manganyi, "Continuity and Change in African Culture: The Writer's Response" (Johannesburg: University of the Witwatersrand Special Senate Lectures, 1980).

4. Noel Manganyi, *Mashangu's Reverie and Other Essays* (Johannesburg: Ravan Press, 1977), p. 20.

5. Modikwe Dikobe, *The Marabi Dance* (London: Heinemann, 1973).

6. See, for example, Daniel Kunene, *Heroic Poetry of the Basotho* (London: Oxford, 1971); Trevor Cope, *Izibongo: Zulu Praise Poems* (London: Oxford, 1968) amongst others.

7. Timothy Couzens, "The New African," (University of the Witwatersrand Ph.D. Dissertation, 1980).

8. Richard Rive, "Books by Black Writers" (unpublished manuscript). In this regard see also Timothy Couzens, *op. cit.* and "The Continuity of Black Literature in South Africa before 1950," *English in Africa*, 1, No. 2, (1974), pp. 11–23.

9. Notable here are Sol Plaatje's *Mhudi* and Thomas Mofolo's *Chaka*.

10. See Anthony Sampson, *Drum: A Venture into the New Africa* (London: Collins, 1956).

11. Here must be included Peter Abraham's *Return to Goli, Tell Freedom;* Ezekiel Mphahlele's *Down Second Avenue,* Alfred Hutchinson's *Road to Ghana,* Todd Matshikiza's *Chocolates for My Wife,* and Bloke Modisane's *Blame Me on History.*

12. This period is marked mainly by the publication in 1971 of Oswald Mtshali's *Sounds of a Cowhide Drum.* This was followed by the production of numerous books of poetry such as Wally Serote's *Yakhal 'inKomo* and *Tsetlo* amongst others. There are several other poets who published works during this period and later such as Sipho Sepamla, Mafika Gwala and James Mathews.

13. See Mweli Skota, *The African Yearly Register: Being an illustrated Bibliographical Dictionary* (who's who) *of Black Folks in Africa* (Johannesburg, 1930). In his analysis of the brief biographies of the 30s, Timothy Couzens in *The New African, op. cit.,* p. 19, points out that there were eighty-five biographies in which "at least eight formulae emerge: the words 'progressive,' 'hard worker,' 'good speaker,' 'gentleman' and 'true Christian,' or other minor variants appear frequently, as do the ideas of 'taking a kin interest in the social, political, educational and religious welfare of his people,' being concerned for the education of either his own children or that of his people, and finally, that a man is a friend of or respected by 'Europeans.' "

14. See Noel Manganyi, "The Censored Imagination," *English in Africa*, 6, No. 2, (1979), pp. 24–32.

15. At the time of writing, three other autobiographies have come to light. One is N. Mogatle's *Autobiography of an Unknown South African* (1971), followed at the beginning of the eighties by Richard Rive's *Writing Black: An Author's Notebook* and Z. K. Mathews's *Freedom for my People* (1981), the former to be brought out soon by David Philip. In the realm of biography proper, the author's work in progress on Ezekiel Mphahlele appears to his knowledge to be the first major sustained effort in biography by a South African black. Of historical significance is a longish pamphlet entitled *Ntsikana: The Story of an African Convert* (1914), written by John Knox Bokwe. There are, of course, several life studies of blacks in Southern Africa written by non-blacks, such as Hilda Kuper's *Sobhuza II* (1978), which are not our concern in this paper.

16. Wright Mills, *The Sociological Imagination* (London: Oxford, 1959), p. 161; p. 3.

Five Types
of Contemporary French Biography

GABRIEL MERLE

The biographical genre is very productive in France, but it does not inspire much criticism. Systematic studies are rare. And naturally when
a production is not stimulated by some regular critical input, it remains a mere collection of books. That is why, as my cautious title suggests, I cannot claim to give a firmly structured study of the whole picture, although the separate books I am going to examine represent as
large a range of biographical interest as I could find, and although it is
possible to relate them to a single individual influence.

The successive steps of my exposé will be: (1) biography as a natural
flow; (2) biography as temptation; (3) biography as reconquest; (4) biography as crowning; and (5) biography as subversion. These are the
labels which I found could be attached to Jean Lacouture's *François
Mauriac*, Philippe Beaussant's *Le Biographe (The Biographer)*, Claude
Manceron's *Les Hommes de la Liberté (Freedom's Men)*, Marc Soriano's
Jules Verne, and Daniel Bertaux's *Histoires de Vies—ou Récits de Pratiques? (Life Histories—or Narratives of Practical Experiences?)* respec-
tively.

1. Biography as Natural Flow

Lacouture's *Mauriac* (1980) may be called classical. I was tempted to
call it "traditional." But you would have reminded me of the theme of
this symposium: "New Directions in Biography." And it is true that to
a certain extent the book gives a New Direction. To what we shall see.

François Mauriac, novelist and dramatist, saw himself as an off-
spring of our classical drama, especially Racine's. Elected to the *Acadé-
mie Française* in 1933, at the comparatively early age of 48, Nobel Prize
in 1952 at 67, he had a brilliant literary career.

His spiritual and political itinerary was not so straight. A practising
Catholic, a conservative, he adopted more than once progressive, leftist

positions. He resisted the Nazis; he was against revenge at the liberation; he protested against torture in Algeria; in a word he was advocate of the oppressed and humiliated. His main weapon was his pen—he was a redoubtable pamphleteer.

This biography is the first of Mauriac in French. Technically, it is copious; it comes out at a reasonable distance from the writer's death (ten years); it has benefitted from the ungrudging help of the family; it is classical in the sense that the arrangement of letters, documents, quotations is of a traditional type; it is a "critical biography": life and work unfold simultaneously. Ethically it is discreet. Mauriac is shown with some defects; not too many—rather, he is the good father and good husband. A pamphlet of 1954 against his early private life is called "vile" but not quoted. During a television programme, Lacouture was asked if he practised autocensorship: "No," he said, "I am a prudish man, so I am myself when I write like this."

But in its general thrust, the book has something definitely new: the pamphleteer is privileged in comparison with the writer. Here we have the biographer *placing his full weight on the interpretation of men and their times*. Mauriac was for me what Hugh Kingsmill was for Michael Holroyd—he made literature real to me. But the average reader of the future will derive from this book the vision of a man with a profound sense of justice rather than the image of a remote heir of Racine probing the depths of modern hearts.

A journalist himself, involved in politics, Lacouture may have had personal reasons to focus his book on Mauriac's political and journalistic work; he may also be one of those who think Mauriac's aesthetics are outdated. But he had an objective justification: this upper-middle class man, throwing the weight of his fame into political battles, did indeed have a real political and moral influence.

So, we see Mauriac from an angle certainly new to the student of literature. The book also lays stress on two points—the intellectual in a situation of rupture with his milieu and the man of letters leaving his ivory tower—which certainly represent a certain novelty in biography. But this connection seems to be unconscious. *François Mauriac* appears as a sample of those biographies which will be written anyway by able practitioners, unconcerned with a new methodology or epistemological problems. It is biography as natural flow.

2. Biography as Temptation

Beaussant's book (1978) is remarkably short—132 pages only. It depicts a historian who is studying the Congress of Vienna of 1814–1815.

Here is an example of the kind of question he asks himself: "Why did the German princelings adopt French policy so easily?" In order to answer such questions, he searches for unknown documents, or unknown archives; he consults the memoirs of one of Talleyrand's emissaries, the Marquess of St. Anthelme. Now, the Marquess's memoirs show a blank of two weeks—between December 20, 1814 and January 4, 1815, the day when the secret treaty was signed. Then, gradually, files and archives give way to more personal documents. The historian has left the large avenues of history for its little lanes. Asking himself again the obsessive question "What was exactly St. Anthelme's mission? What were Talleyrand's instructions to him?" he suddenly answers with excitement: "It doesn't matter and I don't care a fig."

What matters for him is the love-story he has just discovered between St. Anthelme and the young wife of an old French ambassador, and especially the young woman's personality and her awakening to life: the historian begins to feel some fondness for living creatures. Cleopatra's nose is worth looking at after all. The heroine takes hold of him. He goes as far as saying "I hate history." He has turned biographer (you recollect it is the title of the book).

But that is not all.

Apart from two perfectly genuine documents (a letter from King Louis XVIII and another from Talleyrand) the rest is pure fiction. The subtitle is *A Narrative.* The author told me he had proposed *A Novel,* which the publisher ruled out—and yet that was just the connection Philippe Beaussant wanted to show.

During the long conversation I had with him, he confirmed to me that his fundamental question was, "How can I establish a link between the hard facts, the documents, and the resuscitation of man?"— which is also one of our questions here.

His answer is that history cannot restore life. Biography can. (In this little book, the medium is a "novel," but it is a provisional medium.) The dialectal bonds existing between biography and fiction are strong, they are not fortuitous: 1. Every biography—insofar as it is the quest for meaningful behaviour—tends to the imaginary (the French archetypes might well be Sartre's biographies of Genet and Flaubert). 2. Every fiction, insofar as it explores Time and deciphers the mystery of an individual psychology in action, is related to biography.

This "biographical temptation" was real: Philippe Beaussant, two years after his *Biographer,* published the life of the French musician François Couperin, and the choice is probably not accidental; for Couperin's life is one about which little is known, and for which the biographer must needs recreate. Beaussant had succumbed to the seduction of biography.

This book exemplifies—without a word of theory—the problem of the imbrication of the three genres, history, fiction, biography; and affirms that the last one is best suited to make us feel the throbbing of life.

3. Biography as Reconquest

Manceron's books pose the problem of the interrelationship of history and biography.

There used to be a time when history included biography. The past then comprised the lives of great men. Then a past of events and ideas was gradually worked out, more and more independent of the lives of the actors. The name of history was kept for those general considerations, and individual histories were christened biography. (And you may recollect that the godfather, Dryden, was not very ambitious for his goddaughter.)

But there always were historians longing for biography. In 1834, Michelet wrote in his diary: "Intimate methods—biographize history, as of a man, as of myself." However, positivist historians, and later Marxists and structuralists in their turn, tended to study history in terms of abstract forces. Then in 1962 Claude Lévi-Strauss, although a structuralist himself, wrote:

> Biographical and anecdotical history is less explanatory but is richer from the point of view of information . . . The choice a historian has to make is always between a history which teaches more and explains less and a history which explains more and teaches less.

Manceron availed himself of these cautions on the first page of his book, whose subtitle is "Exploration of the roots of the French Revolution through the medium of interlocked biographies." "Interlocked biographies" is the key phrase.

The project is to go from 1774 to 1797 (hardly a quarter of a century). Originally, eight books were planned. They became ten; four of them have already been published. At the present rate, *Freedom's Men* will amount to six to seven thousand pages: biographical history is rarely economical.

In Volume I only *(The King at 20, 1774–78),* over five hundred people are dealt with; most of them French of course, but also Englishmen, Prussians, Austrians, Russians, and Americans. They represent people appearing in traditional history, but also philosophers, writers, artists, scientists, *and* much less exalted people, humble people who at one given moment found themselves caught in the meshes of history.

It reads like a day-to-day memorandum book of some European—or even world-wide—family. The impression of life is prodigious, inasmuch as the author uses all kinds of styles. But most important for us is that events and ideas are ascribed and attached to this or that man, and *not* to the spirit of the age (which is unpredictable during a revolutionary period, when ideas change very often). In other words, biography and history become one and the same thing.

Insofar as this method deals with everyday life and biographical elements, it is practised by other French historians, such as Braudel and Le Roy Ladurie. Le Roy Ladurie writes, "There is no shortage of broad synthesis; what is sometimes lacking is the direct look, the evidence without intermediary, without go-between."

I have chosen to speak at some length of Manceron because his is the largest and boldest venture, and exclusively biographical. What he is doing is really the biography of a generation. It is the borderline case of group biography. With him, biography reconquers its former role of privileged vehicle of history.

Yet, it is not a mere return to an old situation, for two reasons: 1. If one recollects what Lévi-Strauss said of explaining and teaching, it looks as if Manceron had taken this as a challenge and accepted it; for he manages to explain as much as he teaches. 2. Returning to biography also means listening to the humble ones: it has become a democratic approach.

4. Biography as Coronation

The name of Jules Verne is associated with narratives of travels, especially imaginary ones, and to more or less fantastic adventures with a scientific basis. This kind of literature was left alone by the critics for quite a long time. The turn of the tide began after World War II. Since then, there have been many studies about Verne and his work, and from different angles. Marc Soriano's book is one of the latest.

That book matured slowly. Soriano studied Jules Verne with his students and his colleagues in the classroom and in various seminars (Limoges 1972–73; Stanford 1973–75; Paris 7 University 1975–78).

The challenge was that the man Verne was apparently banal and problemless (the good husband, good father again). Soriano, however, spots and tracks down inconsistencies in the portrait. For instance: from the political angle, Verne was a "democrat" and considered as such—but there are traces of racism in him; from the psychological angle, Verne loved women and appreciated them—but there hovers in his book the recurrent figure of a glamorous youth; from the angle of writing, his work is eminently clear and readable—but it is full of bizarre names, anagrams, cryptograms, spoonerisms (and so are his private papers).

Soriano undertakes to go and see behind these contradictions. Following the history track, he replaces Verne in his time in order to arrive at a political interpretation of the man. Following the linguistic track, he deciphers and interprets thousands of neologisms. (One of the most original parts of the book is a glossary of these words, and the study of Verne's procedures for coding them.) Following the psychoanalytical track, he concludes Verne was bisexual, with latent homosexuality. He thinks the machines and elements which fill his books were "substitute women," the machines having this characteristic of being delicate, a bit dangerous, and of enabling men to travel between men.

Soriano's final ambition, repeatedly expressed, was to find how Verne's imaginary world functioned, and to discover "his little inner cinema hidden behind the linguistic stereotypes of his times."

Using the tools of such neighbouring disciplines as history, linguistics, and psychoanalysis is not really new. But one great novelty is the team work: oral questions to, and discussions with, seminar participants, and frontal, though by no means passive, use of other—often prominent—scholars' work. This biography is the opposite of those naive biographies, written as if writing a life was a matter of course. It is a quest, an inquiry, nearly a police investigation, conducted by Superintendent Soriano, with the help of a number of detectives, whose occasional finds he acknowledges with remarkable honesty.

The other great novelty of this biography is its attitude to chronology and to aesthetic judgment. "Biography," Soriano says, "has its phantasms: the registry office is one of them, and the work of art is another." "Now," he adds, "this Biography is the meeting point of two phantasms: the author's and ours. Jules Verne is a sensitized [photographic] plate reflecting our own image."

Soriano frees himself from the chronological "phantasm," and he frees himself from the aesthetic "phantasm": his chronology is annexed to the narrative, and he passes no aesthetic judgment on Verne's work.

Finally he says "This biography is full of facts but it is not factual; it involves historical work but it is not historical; it involves psychoanalysis but it is not psychoanalytical. It is not sociological either. It is anthropological." That is why one can speak of a scientific, interdisciplinary biography. Of course, as part of the bargain it is literary too.

Biography has been called a Cinderella. In the present case, there are many people at her service. Cinderella has turned Queen, and been crowned.

5. Biography as Subversion

Question 7 of the questionnaire preparatory to this Symposium was: Do you think there have been important recent changes in the interrelationship between biography and other fields such as psychology and the social sciences?

In France, the answer is emphatically yes. About fifteen years ago, sociology and philosophy were dominated by the positivists (or neopositivists), the Marxists, and the structuralists. What these had in common was the belief that men are totally determined, that they are the products of circumstances, and that consequently what is interesting is to study the circumstances.

They didn't take man into account. Thus, sociologists were building a purely quantitative science, based on a theoretical discourse, not on observation. Some used the survey research, or School of Columbia method, but several young sociologists found themselves ill at ease in that sociology. Like Studs Terkel, they found the survey research method more "closed" than "open," and they resisted the opinion of one of their brilliant elders, Pierre Bourdieu, for whom in such inquiries the necessary postulate was the non-consciousness of the questioned.

In 1964, one of them, Daniel Bertaux, happened to read *The Children of Sanchez,* which made a considerable impact on him. Having also read C. Wright Mills' *The Power Elite,* he thought there was something to be said for biography as a technique of sociological investigation. The life history technique is not new. It was practised in Chicago more than fifty years ago, by Thomas and Znaniecki. But their book, *The Polish Peasant,* was not known in France. Bertaux began experimenting under the influence of Oscar Lewis alone. He read books systematically and worked out his theory later.

He chose for his first subject the bakery trade—not a social group, not an age group, but a production sector. Unlike other countries of Western Europe, in France the small family shop has not been eliminated by industrial production. And it is his report we are examining now.

Bertaux soon discovered that, contrary to what he had been taught, those bakers—shop-owners, workers, workers having acquired a shop, bakers' wives—were all extremely conscious of social relationships. It was only through those long, attentive, numerous interviews that he was able to understand why the family trade had survived. He became convinced it had been a mistake for the social sciences to take a model in the exact sciences. It was high time they returned to real empiricism. For his part, he decided to use biography systematically.

However, he had his own objections to the "biographical fact": 1. He rejects the cliché that there is everywhere a universal discourse on Man, Life, and Destiny. A society he says is based on power. There are the rulers and the ruled. The former alone can develop their personalities freely. When the ruling class speaks of equality, it is an imposture. It is the imposture of traditional humanism. 2. He finds everywhere the postulate of the unity of a life. False, he says. It is a metaphysical postulate. This unitarian conception is based on the romantic concept of the hero. One must get rid of the biographical ideology, and admit there is such a thing as distinct sections in a life, with distinct social relationships. For example, a life of Kerensky, the political man, should stop around 1920. 3. He wants to get rid of blind determinism. Man he claims is *not* a mere product of relationships, the mere carrier of a structure. Neither is he pure will power. He is the seat of a dialectical process in which the determined creature surpasses itself by practising. In this line he is admittedly helped by Jean-Paul Sartre, who expressed his own conception of freedom in the famous formula: man makes something out of what was made of him. 4. Bertaux has another, respectable, fear. He knows that ethnological investigations reinforced imperialism; that missionaries' reports did the same; that the State relief given to the immigrants after Thomas and Znaniecki's research at the beginning of the century only perpetuated the immigrants' dependence. And that when giving the humble a chance to make their own lives meaningful by relating it, one is not sure to do them good. But he concludes that the risk is worth taking. Biography can be the basis of a new sociology. By intimately mixing observation and theory, by posing clearly the questions "by whom? about whom? for whom?" it can entirely renew the way of working—and the way of living—of the researchers, and sociology itself. The result: a sociology free from intellectual terrorism, and consequently more democratic.

Whether biography—or, often, autobiography—which is servant of a social science, is publishable, and so a matter of interest for us biographers, is of course open to debate. But the interest is not I think at the production level. It is the theoretical affirmation of the importance of biography that matters. Here was a proud science which tended to be all patterns, diagrams, equations, and to obliterate individuals and their lives. Then one of its devotees rises up to say forcefully: sociology needs men. Social relationships, which it is the job of a sociologist to find, are invisible though they underlie the lives of men. They will be found only if men themselves are allowed to speak.

Bertaux himself says biography *subverted* his former practice. He is no longer alone on this line. There exists today a "Life History approach network" including 124 sociologists representing twenty-four countries from East and West: for all of them, the little servant biography has taken over.

But there are other aspects to the problem. The readers of *Biography* know that in a recent issue (III:1, 1980) Freeman and Krantz wrote very reticently on the subject of Life History: "After sixty years of promise, the 'potential' of Life History is yet to be fulfilled."

That Freeman and Bertaux do not know each other is clear and understandable. What is more surprising is that they don't read the same books. Bertaux's bibliography contains 84 books, Freeman's 45. Only three titles appear in both lists. Besides, none of the 124 researchers working in the Bertaux network is known to Freeman.

It seems we are in front of a quarrel between two antagonistic schools. The question that arises here is: is it our problem? Do we have to take sides? A close study shows that on some points it will not be impossible to bridge the gap between them, but when Freeman maintains "it is a life in its entirety that is distinctive—which is the "biographical ideology," or the "traditional humanistic attitude" denounced by Bertaux—the gap seems unbridgeable; and it seems difficult for us to wash our hands of the conflict.

Unless, of course, one chooses to ignore the divergences and say that beyond the differences between the traditional use of biography and Bertaux's new anthroponomical methods, the important element is the presence of man—or should we say "men." The adoption of the plural would be the sign of the rejection of the concept of personality which characterized the humanism of old. It is in that, anyway, that Bertaux parts from Sartre, in whom he finds what he calls traces of bourgeois humanism. A Sartre who, however, greatly influenced him—as he very explicitly wrote.

Sartre's interests in biography are more important than it would seem. At first, he rejected it as being impossible (*La nausée*, 1938).

"The Biographee," he said, "does not need a Biographer," . . . "it is the Biographer who wants to run away from his own life."

Then he accepted it, or rather declared it necessary, as "an attempt to bring existing and being into coincidence." But his problem was: how is it possible not to betray the subject's freedom? Freedom was the key word with him.

Sartre was led successively to reject Marxism and Freudism—or go beyond; Marxism as neglecting childhood and lacking in prospect; Freudism as looking too exclusively for the traumas of childhood. For him, Man (notice the singular) is neither subject, nor object, but project.

In order to reconstruct this project, to discover what he calls the tension of a life, he constantly establishes a back and forth movement between past, present, and future, a technique he called progressive-regressive, and which is to be found at its clearest in his Genet or his Flaubert.

All his effort is to preserve—difficult as it is—the balance between the knowledge of the one who writes and the freedom of the one who is written about. That is what he expresses in a beautiful formula: "Man's function is to create—or to invent Man."

The influence of Sartre on the five authors I have been studying is either diffuse, or explicit, but always real. Its measurement would of course require a specific study.

But let's come back to the heading of this Symposium, "New Directions in Biography." In this brief survey of five types of French biography at the beginning of the '80s, I have tried to show that it was living, and also that it did open new vistas:

—either because it was able to tempt a novelist;

—or because it compelled recognition, from historians and sociologists;

—or because it was considered a serious discipline, deserving to be at the centre of an interdisciplinary research.

So there is cause for biography and biography-lovers to rejoice. We rejoice for two reasons:

—It is naturally pleasant to see one's trade thriving.

—The second reason is deeper. "Good biography," one of the contributors to the questionnaire said, is *ipso facto* culturally constructive." How true! As for me, I shall say: Man—or men, if we adopt the change—are in perpetual danger of being flattered or belittled, deified or reified, crushed or denied or forgotten by some power or other—

political, religious, or (sad as it is to say) intellectual, not to speak of the formidable power of Father Time. Now rejoicing in the vitality of biography is not turning our backs on science: the elaborate constructions of men's minds are priceless. But so are the sounds of their laughter and the beatings of their hearts.

BIBLIOGRAPHY

BEAUSSANT, Philippe.   *Le Biographe*, NRF, 1978
BERTAUX, Daniel.   *Histoire de Vies—ou Récits de Pratiques? Méthodologie de l'approche biographique en Sociologie*, Typescript, 1976
LACOUTURE, Jean.   *François Mauriac;* Seuil, 1980
MANCERON, Claude.   *LES HOMMES DE LA LIBERTE*, Robert Laffont
                          1 *Les Vingt ans du Roi* (1774–1778) 1972
                          2 *Le Vent d'Amérique* (1778–1782) 1974
                          3 *Le Bon Plaisir* (1782–1785) 1976
                          4 *La Révolution qui lève* (1785–1787) 1979
Le ROY LADURIE, E.   *Montaillou, village occitan* de 1294 à 1324, Gallimard, 1975
SORIANO, Marc.   *Jules Verne*, Julliard, 1978
Cahiers de l'Association Internationale des Etudes Françaises,
n° 19 (mars 1967)   (Roman et biographie après le XVIIIe s.) pp. 85–166
SARTRE, J. P.   *La nausée*, NRF, 1938
                          Situations, III, NRF, 1949
                          Baudelaire, NRF, 1947
                          Saint Genet, comédien et martyr, NRF, 1952
                          L'idiot de la famille, NRF, 1971
                          L'être et le néant, NRF, 1943
                          Critique de la Raison dialectique, NRF, 1960

The Curious Relationship Between Biography and Autobiography in Japan

SHOICHI SAEKI

1

A few months ago in Japan we started a major publishing project, "Compilations of Japanese Autobiographies," in which we plan to include no less than seventy modern autobiographies within twenty-three volumes plus two additional volumes (some of the pre-modern autobiographies, and biographical commentaries, included). I happen to be one of the two general editors for this series, and I admit this is a rather risky, though ambitious, project. We have neither a grant nor a subsidy from any foundation to depend upon. Our publisher is not a university press. This is a purely "commercial" series, intended for the general public. We have published only the first two volumes, but, so far, the general response has turned out very good. Though we should not be too optimistic, we hope and believe we will be able to accomplish this "tour de force" within two years or so.

One of the reasons for our optimism should be called literary or cultural rather than economic. We felt we could depend upon the ingrained predilection for "personal" writings on the part of the Japanese readers. I am not sure whether this taste or liking is a cultural virtue or vice. We have tended to overindulge ourselves in this taste for many centuries. It may be we have had enough or already too much of "personal" writings in Japan. My definition of "personal" writings is rather wide and miscellaneous. It includes not only many short lyrical poems such as *waka* and *haiku* but also *zuihitsu* (essays) and particularly autobiographical writings, which started as "nikki" around the 10th and 11th centuries. I do not want to dwell upon the historical details, but should like to point out that all these forms of "personal" expression were not merely passing fashions, but have stayed alive. Not one of them has been discarded, and all continue to be practiced and enjoyed as living literary media.

The case of "nikki" is especially interesting and illuminating in the context of our present theme. "Nikki" means diary or journal, and one of the earliest examples happened to be a travel diary, but the Japanese readers of the 10th century were willing to accept it as literature, preserve and transmit it, as part of the literary classics, to posterity. They did not seem to be worried about the literary legitimacy of such an apparently factual record of personal life. The writer of this "nikki" was a famous *waka* poet who played the witty trick of writing under the disguise of an anonymous female. This trick might have had something to do with the book's literary success. But his adopted mask was rather thin and not hard to look through. The contemporary readers seemed to have appreciated the "personal" quality of the "nikki" for its own sake. Quite a few writers followed his example—including the authoress of the *Tale of Genji*—and spontaneously enough, the daily record of a private life grew into a life story or memoir.

There were several remarkable points about this early emergence of autobiographical writing as an accepted literary genre in Japanese literature. The first point was, of course, its early date. Indeed there was already St. Augustine's *Confessions*. But these Japanese diaries were utterly secular, having nothing to do with religious ritual or duty. Besides, they were almost exclusively concerned with the private aspect of the lives portrayed. They did not pretend to social significance; their main emphasis was upon their subjects' domestic lives and emotional and psychological responses—disappointments in love, matrimonial hardships becoming their central topics. Not *what* they *did*, but *how* they *felt* was regarded as more important, more worth recording by these female autobiographers. In that sense, they could be called forerunners of the modern romantic egotist. They might be defined as a group of female minor Rousseaus. Indeed they did anticipate European romanticists by eight or nine centuries.

With so much concern over personal emotion, such an intense preoccupation with the private aspect of life, it should be natural for us to expect the simultaneous or imminent emergence of "biography" in Japan. But, unfortunately, no! In spite of numerous remarkable autobiographies and in spite of *Tale of Genji*, a masterpiece so rich in psychological nuances, biography was very slow in developing. Of course, there were historical narratives, remarkable for their variety and dexterity in character sketches, written almost contemporaneously with *Tale of Genji*, such as *Okagami* ("Great Mirror") and even a romance-

memoir of an eminent aristocrat, Fujiwara Michinaga, who was regarded as a model for the central character, the so-called Shining
Prince of *Tale of Genji.* Michinaga's domestic happiness and achievements as an administrator were eulogized with colorful rhetoric in *Ei-
gamonogatari* ("A Story of Glorious Prosperity"). However, although
the social and political prerequisites for biography were there, one was
too fragmentary, and the other marred by too sentimental nostalgia. Japan of the 11th century, which could boast herself as a "mature society," both politically and culturally, remained stable and undis-
turbed for almost two hundred years. And although its aristocrats did
not seem particularly efficient, being—from the literary point of view—
devoted to the pleasures of love-making and elaboration of *waka,* it is
really difficult for us to find any other century as rich and refined, as
active and luxuriant. However, we do miss one genre—biography.

2

External conditions seemed quite ready for it. But still, it did not
come. Why? Some clues have already been given. Cultural aristocrats
of Heian Japan believed in the value of private life, and became obsessed with the emotional and psychological complexities of human relationships. Hence, so many autobiographies and fine novels. But they
were written almost exclusively by *female* authors. Male aristocrats
were expected or required to write in Chinese, the orthodox, official
language of the time, and the use of native Japanese for literary purposes (except *waka*) was regarded with suspicion, as beneath them.
This linguistic discrimination turned out favorable for the non-elite,
under-privileged of that period, that is, female authors. They could be
free from the literary burden of adopted Chinese culture, and could be
spontaneous and express their emotional selves through the native medium. They could compose poems, romances, novels, autobiographies,
and even essays. But, somehow, *no* biographies. Heian Japan was immersed in new enthusiasm for Mahayana Buddhism; and, naturally
enough, there were written some elaborate hagiographies, biographies
of famous saints or priests such as one finds by Christians in the European Middle Ages. Their style was fine, but altogether too conventional, conforming to the preconceived pattern of piety and devotion
derived from Indian originals.

Biography *precedes* autobiography—this seems to be the general rule
of literary development in most cultures. And, so far as the emergence
of a secular type of autobiography is concerned, we usually have to
wait a long time, even after the biographical genre has come into its

own. Reticence and moral scruples delayed the process in Japan, as they did in Europe and New England, where in the early years one found many pious autobiographies but little or nothing in the way of secular autobiography. It really needed a psychological and spiritual breakthrough for bold self-disclosure to be carried through. It needed the crazy genius of J. J. Rousseau.

Broadly speaking, autobiography could be characterized as a modern, Western institution, while biography could boast of many ancient classical predecessors. It should be very hard for us to find even an embryonic autobiography before Plutarch or Ssu-ma Ch'ien, while we need not seek far to come across a group of excellent autobiographies, after Johnson, Boswell, or J. G. Lockhart. It could be claimed that the biographical genre paved the way for the emergence of autobiography. As the term suggests, auto + biography (a new coinage of early 19th century) might be defined as a technical application of the biographical method to a life writing of one's own, a new superstructure built upon the groundwork of biography.

However, this general rule, this course of literary development, does not apply to Heian Japan where autobiography preceded biography— emerged on the scene, as it were, on its own. Indeed, biography was relatively late in coming to Japan, although Ssu-ma Ch'ien remained one of the favorite Chinese authors of Japanese literary intellectuals for many centuries, starting with the authoress of *Genji*. We have to wait until as late as the 17th century before we come across any biographical writing worth the name. It was only after Japan went through the century of "internal wars" (which covered more than a century, from the middle of the 15th to the latter half of the 16th century) that we had an entire book devoted to the life story of one of the most flamboyant military leaders of those turbulent years. This biography, Ohta Gyūichi's *Records of Prince Nobunaga,* proved a breakthrough, and many other books similar in pattern and technique, dealing with other *samurai*—Nobunaga's military rivals and others—followed. Some of the successful biographies of this period remained so popular and could make the features and deeds of these *samurai* heroes so familiar to the general public, that even today we come across the application of their basic pattern and motifs in the television serials.

However, these life stories of *samurai* heroes were quite a new growth, utterly unrelated to the foregoing autobiographies of Heian ladies. They were the cultural products of a different age and different temperaments—even of a different world-view. The new biographers of the 17th century did not owe any of their techniques, ways of presentation and characterization to those female aristocratic authors. From the literary point of view, they were too crude and naive, lacking emotional delicacy and psychological shades. We should not, however, underrate their new contribution: the firm grasp of the military reality; the vivid and lively description of men in action; and the straightforward characterization or *samurai* heroes in bold outline.

So we must ask the same question again. Why was it that Heian female writers succeeded in creating their autobiographies out of the void, as it were? How was it possible they could talk of their own private life, their hidden emotions and excitements so candidly, so fearlessly? They did not seem to be troubled with any moral scruples, with any sense of social decency. They looked very modern, liberated, and sophisticated—though, in actual life, they suffered greatly from the male chauvinistic *moeurs* of Heian society. They disclosed their humiliations, jealousies, and ecstasies with self-confidence. And Heian readers seemed to have accepted those bold self-disclosures without any reservations and to have appreciated them fully as legitimate literature. The characteristics of the Heian milieu would seem most fitting for the cultivation of the biographical sense—a sense of human beings as internal, psychological entities, and the perception of variety and variability of human characters. But, actually, the painful ordeal of a "hundred-year civil war" was needed for the Japanese biography to come into its own. The psychological concern and an emotional preoccupation with self was there. But it was not enough.

3

From biography to autobiography—this order was, as we have seen, reversed in Japanese literature. What caused this exceptional reversal? It is a big, fundamental question. To answer it, we will need more space, more far-reaching historical research than I will try to give. But here are some tentative answers.

1. The *quality* of self-consciousness on the part of Heian autobiographers should have something to do with it. It was highly emotional rather than intellectual or philosophical. It was intense, but narrow. It put considerable emphasis upon mood and atmosphere and aspired toward a lyrical ecstasy.

2. It was intensely concerned with the *private* aspect of life—almost to the neglect of the public domain. For the authoress of *Kagero Nikki* ("Gossamer Diary"), for example, the public career of her not-too-faithful husband meant almost nothing, though he happened to be a Prime Minister (and a very competent one) for some years. She did not

even mention the fact. What mattered to her was whether he remained faithful and passionate or not. She was a mistress of the intimate—a thorough-going personalist. Her consistency all throughout her autobiography was remarkable, something admirable; and her ability to express herself was brilliant, although we cannot expect her to compose a trustworthy biography even of her own husband.

3. This neglect of the public domain (at least as a literary subject) was not limited to the authoress of *Kagerô Nikki*. It was not merely a personal mania of her own. It formed the cultural ambience of Heian Japan, even the aesthetic cannon, which continued to prevail even after Heian aristocracy broke down. This personal purism, as it were, this intense concentration upon the private, emotional aspect of life, could be detected still at work even among the contemporary novelists, such as Kafû Nagai, Yasunari Kawabata, Junichirô Tanizaki, *etc.*

So the abrupt emergence of *samurai* biographies in the 17th century should be taken as a reaction to this prevalent cult of intimacy on the part of public-domain-oriented writers. Indeed, it was an inevitable and salutary reaction. But it remained naive and one-sided, to the neglect of the emotional depth and psychological acumen of Heian autobiographers. The biographers of the 17th century were preoccupied with the external deeds of the military activists, and excited and intoxicated with their subjects' bloody feats and triumphs. They tended to romanticize and idolize their military heroes too easily, and, most of their biographies could not exceed the literary level of historical romances, didactic entertainment, though some of the short biographies by Arai Hakuseki (1657–1725) were exceptionally good, reminding us of the precise, sharp effects of Tacitus. It was not a mere coincidence that Hakuseki happened to be one of the finest *samurai* autobiographers. He was one of the few Japanese intellectuals who could bring the *samurai* ethos and psychological finesse into harmony. His prose, both in his biographies and autobiography, was supple and sinewy, delicate and vigorous at the same time.

4

However, Arai Hakuseki was one of the happy few. The gap between Heian autobiographers and *samurai* biographers turned out too wide, even unbridgeable. Feminine emphasis upon emotional delicacy and introspection, on the one hand, and masculine dedication to public value, military action on the other; the endless psychological circle of narcissism versus a preoccupation with the ethical code, even to the practice of self-sacrifice *(seppuku);* an apex of pure emotionalism versus a glorification of *samurai* stoicism. These listings of contrasts could be lengthened. It was more than the battle of the sexes, more than the collision of the different temperaments, at least for the Japanese writers. You might complain of the contrived artificiality of this gap, this opposition of values. Heian female autobiographers and *samurai* biographers lived and wrote in different ages, so many centuries apart; they were just different tribes, literary antipodes. But the Japanese showed exceptional perseverance not only in preserving but also sticking to their traditional cultural values and codes. Heian authoresses would force their emotional aestheticism and standard of refined taste upon succeeding writers for many centuries, and the *samurai* code of honor, with its behavior pattern, glorified and systematized to its fastidious detail by the biographers of the 17th century and following, did not lose its subtle fascination even after the Japanese were exposed to the impact of Western modernization. Many modern biographies of "national heroes"—mainly, generals and admirals who proved their military strategy and valor through the Sino-Japanese (1894–95) and the Russo-Japanese (1904–5) wars—were composed after those *samurai* models, and even their technical successes were explained in terms of the *samurai* spirit. (*Bushidô* was adopted as a favorite catchword by so many of the Meiji biographers.) But one of the most recent and flamboyant examples of this magical enchantment of the *samurai* ideal was Yukio Mishima, who liked so much to talk of *Bumbu-ryôdô* ("That combination or integration of literary and military disciplines," which implies the harmonious synthesis of Heian grace and *samurai* spirit) and who even managed to put it into practice by killing himself in strictly *samurai* style.

But eventually, of course, the modernizing impact began to work upon the Japanese biographers. They started by translating Western biographies of "great men" with enthusiasm, if not with discernment. Some of the popular subjects of these early translations were Washington, Gladstone, Emerson, General Gordon, and Victor Hugo—quite a mixed company; but one of the most successful and influential early translations happened to be Samuel Smiles' *Self Help.* It was translated as *Biographies of Western Men of High Ambition* and immediately became a startling bestseller. The fact that the translator was a celebrated Confucian scholar and educator was symptomatic. Modern pragmatism and an emphasis upon technological efficiency (Smiles, a Scottish surgeon and social reformer, wrote popular biographies of engineers, starting with George Stephenson) were grafted upon Confucian didacticism and the *samurai* code of rigid and energetic self-discipline. A curious combination, indeed, but, somehow, it worked and appealed to the imagination and ambition of Meiji Japanese.

There were also giant, two or three volume commemorative biographies of "successful" politicians and business men. They were obviously planned and composed after the Victorian originals. Victorian respectability and self-complacency were strictly adhered to, though there were many shades of dark political intrigue, corruption, and sexual scandals about those "successful" and "great" men. Politicians of the Meiji era, such as Hirobumi Ito (1841–1909), who rose melodramatically from a low-class *samurai* of the pre-Meiji era to the premiership, and Eiichi Shibusawa (1840–1931), a leading financier and fabulously "prolific" father, were notorious for their sexual exploits and the incredible number of their mistresses, but most of their "respectable" biographers did not even allude to their promiscuity. Meiji biographers followed faithfully their Victorian models—not only in their modernizing zeal but also in their tight-lipped hypocrisy.

Naturally there was a reaction against the Japanese Meiji version of Victorianism. Ryunosuke Akutagawa (1892–1927), the versatile story-teller of "Rashomon," was one of the brightest champions of the "down-with-feudal-and-didactic-hypocrisy" campaign, but his literary output did not include any biographical monograph. His satirical portrait of General Nogi, the most idolized "national hero" of prewar Japan together with Admiral Togo, was cleverly done, but remained rather sketchy and thin. Though we have had not a few novels and biographies in a similar debunking vein by modern authors, we cannot point to any Japanese equivalent of Lytton Strachey.

In this context, we are reminded again of the subtle, persistent fascination emanating from the Heian autobiographers, a perhaps unbroken charmed circle of eternal femininity. So many of the serious, talented Japanese writers seem to have succumbed to the emotional appeal of pure *personal* narrative, and have become obsessed by the autobiographical impulse, which has proved so deeply ingrained, almost hereditary. They write, on and on, autobiographical fragments—even under the vigorous impact of the modern European novel. ("Watakushi shosetsu"—the "I novel"—has become a well-established genre and even part of the indispensable critical jargon in modern Japan.) The I novelists remain self-absorbed, and as narcissistic as their Heian predecessors, being immersed in the rather trivial details of their domestic and literary life. They have preferred to keep themselves aloof and detached, remaining social outsiders—even literary hermits. So biographies and novels with significant social themes have, in many cases, been left to less serious second-raters, sometimes mere shrewd sensationalists. Even last year, one of the most publicized bestsellers happened to be a pseudo-biography, or historical romance of two legendary military leaders of ancient China.

However, we cannot and should not conclude on a negative tone. And indeed there are some positive notes. Recently we have seen a batch of "new biographies"—Hiroyuki Agawa's *Reluctant Admiral*, Saburo Shiroya's *War Criminal*, Kinji Shimada's *Saneyuki Akiyama in America*. The subjects of these biographies happen to be the military and political leaders of pre-war and war-time Japan—that is, fallen idols of old-fashioned nationalism. It was not, however, these new biographers' intentions to restore and eulogize the bygone glory of nationalistic Japan, but to analyze and estimate personalities and achievements in the historical perspective with detachment. All these three subjects of the new biographies came to tragic ends: the first (a general and commander-in-chief in the Japanese Navy) killed in action; the second (a prime minister of the 1930's) executed as a war criminal; the third (a flamboyant naval strategist of the Russo-Japanese War) ending his life as an obscure mystic. But the biographers remained restrained and reticent and tried to analyze the basic structure and significance of the traditional ethos (part of the *samurai* heritage), which underlay their subjects' attitudes as public men, and which, to a certain extent, provided the moral basis for many modern Japanese.

I do not want to claim too much for these new biographies. They are just the beginnings of a new wave. And this new wave, or new movement, it seems to me, aspires toward the difficult goal of integrating the psychological insights of Heian autobiographers with the masculine biographers' preoccupation with public values and the samurai ethos. These biographies were concerned not only with the personalities of their subjects, but also with the underlying communal ethos. Of course, it may not make sense to glorify the collective spirit or values of the past, but it is equally nonsensical to deny their existence and workings, or to denigrate them. There was the dark side and the light side, as it were—a hidden irrational aspect, and an open, bright aspect; blind irrational patterns, and a strict, restraining force. The communal ethos accommodated both sides. We had better observe its intricate working very carefully. Probably we human beings are, at least partly, group animals, emotional animals, and are living under the influence of the group ethos—or, if we borrow the Jungian term, the collective unconscious—more than we are aware of.

Of course, we cannot be too wary of those political or religious leaders who are shrewd enough to make use of this deep-rooted group instinct or mentality of ours, and who try to manipulate us intentionally. On the other hand, frankly speaking, I am becoming sceptical about the concept of pure individualism, and about individuality at any cost, or individuality for its own sake. I am not so sure that individuality can be taken as an ultimate value. Biography as a modern genre, as a European institution, has been developed around the basic concept (and value) of individualism. It has been assumed that the biographical genre should stick to the concept of the individual or of the ego as a basic value. But I should like to ask you to reconsider, or at least, to re-examine this assumption. Especially in the context of Japanese literature, those delicate, intensely emotional Heian autobiographers could hardly be called individualists. They were highly *personal,* but not individualistic in the modern European sense of the word. The samurai biographers of the 17th century could not be labelled individualistic, either, though they were intensely interested in the colorful personalities of their subjects. And in the context of our present theme, "new directions in biography," isn't it high time we put into question the basic assumptions of modern biography and paid more attention to the implicit communal ethos, to supra-individualistic values? Isn't it high time that we grope for ways of going beyond our modern values? Is it beyond us, biographers, to try to add something in our quest for contemporary basic values?

Appendix: Summary of Questionnaire Responses

Biography Symposium: A Questionnaire

1. What are the most important contributions to (a) biographical practice and (b) biographical theory in our century?
2. What books on biography have contributed most to the biographical craft? Have any biographies so contributed?
3. What are the different approaches to biography in different nations? How significant are the major differences?
4. What special biographical insights derive from the culture in which you work that are not to be found elsewhere?
5. Has there been any recent increase in the interchange between biographers from different nations and cultures?
6. How far can biography help focus current cultural and ethical questions and dilemmas?
7. Do you think there have been important recent changes in the interrelationship between biography and other fields such as psychology and the social sciences?
8. What special insights does your particular discipline give to biographical studies?
9. To what extent should biographies be written in conformity with a given social or political theory?
10. Do you see any interrelation between biography and the study of history: or between biography and the study of literature?
11. Have there been any recent important changes in the interrelationship of biography and autobiography?
12. What is the situation of the ghost-writer? Were autobiographies such as those of Eisenhower and Nixon written by ghost or man? Are they the greater or the lesser for being "ghost-written"? What problems do they pose for the biographical historian?
13. What criteria should predominate in the reviewing and criticism of biography?
14. Is it rewarding or futile to discuss the craft of lifewriting and its bearing on an attempt to define and assess contemporary values?

15. Is biography a distinct discipline, or is it an amorphous subject composed primarily of the writing of a few gifted individuals?
16. What new directions do you think biography may take?

Responses to the Questionnaire

The following is a brief summary of the responses to the questionnaire circulated last year among approximately four hundred scholars and writers in the field of biography. The Center received over a hundred responses—varying in length, scope and tone—from widely divergent parts of the world, and from a variety of fields.

A. *The Theory and Practice of Biography.*

The responses made clear what most would suspect: that theory and practice are difficult to separate. Some texts cited in the appended bibliography (see pp. 86–89) are obviously primarily contributions to theory (*e.g.* Leon Edel, *Literary Biography*). But they are also useful practical guides. Others, such as Strachey's *Eminent Victorians,* would seem to have contributed, mostly by example, to the practice of the art. Yet, as many pointed out, they have made a sturdy, if oblique, theoretical impact.

The following were some of the major points which emerged in response to questions 1 and 2. I have tried to arrange these so that the emphasis moves from the practical to the theoretical aspects of the craft—in keeping with a pervading notion among those canvassed that the practical contributions to biography have always been, and still probably are, more important than the theoretical ones.

1. *The modern emphasis on biography as literature.* Some biographers have always accepted their literary responsibilities, argue some of the respondents, but today's writers and readers show an unprecedented awareness of biography's literary potential.

2. *A greater professionalism among biographers.* Many mention the development of biography as a "distinctive genre in its own right" (Norman MacKenzie). This trend is reflected negatively, in the diffidence of some who said that they had only published one or two biographies and would not, therefore consider themselves "biographers."

3. *An increasing inclination to transcend mere chronology.* James Gindin notes a contemporary concern with the poetry and understanding of a subject's personality. And Phillipe Erlanger says, "En résumé, une bonne biographie est celle que montre la formation d'une personalité." (The *formation of personality* is a recurring phrase in the responses.)

4. *A prevailing tolerance—and frank discussion—of human weaknesses* —especially those connected with matters hitherto treated with care, such as sexual and financial affairs. This frankness is partly prompted by the view presented in other responses: that modern biographers benefit from a notion of man as an animal rather than as an emblematic exemplum (Pierson). The Freudian contribution to biographical theory is seen as important here.

Many find modern honesty a mixed blessing. Ronald Duncan, for example, regrets that both theory and practice are dominated by an "unhappy search" for sexual and other deviations which overemphasizes these aspects of life.

5. *A more scrupulous approach to utilizing historical sources.* Simon Karlinsky, for example, sees this as a symptom of the above mentioned honesty. (See also point 9 below—on objectivity).

6. *The availability of superior research aids and sources.* The modern life-writer's concern for accurate and absolute assessment has been accompanied by better research aids: (a) mechanical aids—Xerox, microfilm, computerbanks, photostat, *et al;* (b) better communications—fast and reliable mail, telegrams *etc.;* and (c) more library facilities and cooperation between libraries. Robert Collison, a biographical bibliographer, invokes a professional fantasy when he calls for a "vast biographical bank," allowing immediate computer access to every newly published biographical work.

7. *The growing field of oral history.* Several writers note that oral records add a valuable source. More important, tape and film contribute to the growing interest in the biography of the common man and to "prosopography" or group biography.

8. *Television, film and radio broadcasting.* Such aids mentioned in 6. and 7. beget also means of disbursement. M. C. Bradbrook cites the influence of television as a most important contribution to biographical practice. But, with others, she is wary of "the greed for instrusion fostered by the media."

9. *A current atmosphere of objectivism and relativistic thought.* This is to some extent a corrective against what one respondent called "smarmy" nineteenth century biographies. Our more urbane contemporaries can work in a foreign context without the naiveté and shock frequently seen in earlier, less detached work.

10. *The popularity of the psychological approach.* This trend may be a symptom, a cause, or an accidental concomitant of point 9. A great number of responses assert the theoretical and practical debt to Freud and his disciples, as well as that to Freudian biographers and critics

such as Edel and Erikson. Psychologically informed biography is seen as best when combined with a commitment to biography as art. One writer observes that writers who know psychology are usually more successful biographers than psychologists who write.

11. *The prevailing contribution of traditional literature.* The classics are seen as bearing in two ways: (a) through the application of time-honored standards of biographical criticism and practice (Boswell is often mentioned), and (b) —more obliquely—through the fall-out from Shakespeare's histories and tragedies, *Pilgrim's Progress,* the Bible, Marxist philosophy and so forth. The phrasing of the questionnaire—specifying the contribution to contempory biography—may have caused the writers to pay less attention to pre-twentieth century biographical literature, or to take its impact for granted.

12. *The development of a more extensive theoretical and critical literature about biography.* The assertion of this influence (an impact related to point 2 above) emerged as a complex and contentious matter. First, there are those among the disloyal opposition who said that they knew of little significant theoretical or critical literature. But most of those replying admit the recent increase in such books and articles. Most of the comments on this literature represent three schools: (a) the proponents, who hope "that biographers could now learn some of their craft from existing good books and good critical literature instead of having to re-invent the wheel every time they want to write on someone. . . ." (Lynne Z. Bloom); (b) the opponents, who argue with James Gindin that current theory lags behind practice and that this lag is perhaps useful in preventing formulaic biography "which would sacrifice range and sensitivity for coherence"; and (c) the happy anarchists, who don't think practicing biographers are much influenced by theory. Michael Holroyd put this attitude politely: "I do not believe that books on biography contribute to the biographical craft, but to the craft of literary criticism."

B. *Books Cited as Contributing to Modern Biography*

The following list cites all books mentioned favorably in the responses—usually in relation to questions 1 and 2. It does not, of course, pretend to be a bibliography—even a selective one—of writing in the field.

Respondents either cited specific books (Lytton Strachey's *Eminent Victorians*); subjects (Lytton Strachey on the Victorians and biography); or merely writers (Lytton Strachey's work related to biography). The list obediently follows these differing specifications.

    *   author mentioned more than once
   ** author mentioned more than 3 times
 *** author mentioned more than 5 times

     ACKERLEY, J. R. *Me and my Father*
   * ALTICK, Richard. *Lives and Letters.*
     ARAMNICK, Isaac. *The Rage of Edmund Burke.*
     ARIES, Phillippe. Related writing.
     AUBREY, John. *Lives.*
     BAINTON, Roland. Related writing—especially Freudian criticism of biography.
     BAINVILLE, Jacques. *Napoleon.*
     BALDWIN-SMITH, Lacey. *Henry VIII, The Mask of Royalty.*
     BARRY, Joseph. *Infamous Woman: The Life of George Sand.*
     BATE, W. J. on Keats and *Samuel Johnson.*
     BELL, Quentin. on Woolf.
     BLAKE, Robert. on Disraeli.
     BLUNDEN, Edmund. *Shelley: A Life Story.*
 *** BOSWELL, James. *The Life of Johnson* and all related works.
     BOWRA, Maurice. on himself.
     BOYER and NISSENBAUM. *Salem Possessed.*
   * BRADFORD, Gamaliel. *Biography and the Human Heart.*
     BRITT, Albert. *The Great Biographers.*
     BRODIE, Fawn M. on Jefferson.
     BROMBERT, Beth Archer. on Princess Belgioioso.
     BROWN, Peter. *Augustine of Hippo.*
     BUNYAN, John. *Pilgrim's Progress.*
     BUTLER, Samuel. *Way of All Flesh.*
     CAMERON, James. Related writing.
     CECIL, Lord David. Related writing.
     CLEMENS, Wolfgang. *Der Junge Chaucer.*
 *** CLIFFORD, James. *From Puzzles to Portraits,* and Biographies.
     COLES, Robert. Related writing—especially Freudian criticism of biography.
     COLUMBIA ORAL HISTORY PROJECT.
     DAVIS, David B. "New Directions in American Cultural History," *American Historical Review* LXXIII (February, 1968).
     DEUTSCHER, Isaac. on Trotsky.
     DOBREE, Bonamy. Writing relating to biography.
 *** EDEL, Leon. *Literary Biography* and other work.
 *** EDGAR, Johnson. on Dickens and *One Mighty Torrent: The Drama of Biography.*
     ELLMANN, Richard. Related writing.
 *** ERIKSEN, Erik. *Young Man Luther, Ghandi's Truth, Childhood and Society et al.*
     FRANK, Anne. *The Diary of Anne Frank.*
     FRANK, Joseph. on Dostoevsky.
     FREEMAN, Douglas. on Robert E. Lee and Washington.
 *** FREUD, Sigmund. *et al* (Note: most questionnaires credit modern psychological writers and Freudian critics.)
     FROUDE, James. on Carlyle.

FURBANK, P. N. on E. M. Forster.
* GARRATY, J. A. *The Nature of Biography.*
GEORGE, A. C. and J. L. *Woodrow Wilson and Colonel House.*
GITTINGS, Robert. on Hardy.
GOSSE, Edmund. *Father and Son.*
GRAY, Madeline. *Margaret Sanger.*
GROSSKURTH, Phyllis. on J. A. Symonds and Havelock Ellis.
HAREVEN, Tamara. *Amoskeag.*
HART-DAVIS, Rupert. Related writing.
HIBBERT, Christopher. Related writing.
HOLY BIBLE, The.
* HOLROYD, Michael. on Strachey.
HURD, Michael. *The Ordeal of Ivor Gurney.*
JASPERS, Karl. *Strindberg and Van Gogh,* Hölderlin, Swedenborg, *Nietzsche.*
JONES, Ernest. on Freud.
JOYCE, James. *(Portrait . . .* and *Ulysses).*
KANTOROVICZ, Ernst. *Frederick II.*
* KENDALL, Paul M. *The Art of Biography.*
KLIBANSKY, R., PANOVSKY, E., SAXL, F., *Saturn and Melancholy.*
KUBLER, George. *The Shape of Time.*
LEE, Sidney. *Principles of Biography.*
LEWIS, Oscar. Related writing.
LEWIS, R. W. B. on Edith Wharton.
LOCKHART, John. *Life of Scott.*
LOSSKY, Andrew. on Louis XIV.
LUDWIG, Emil. Related writing.
MACFARLANE, Alan. on Ralph Josselin.
MACK, John. *A Prince of Our Disorder.*
MALONE, Dumas. on Jefferson.
MARAIS, Steven. on Dickens.
MARANON, Gregorio. *Antonio Perez.*
** MARX, Karl (and the Marxists).
*** MAUROIS, André. on Disraeli, Shelley, *Aspects of Biography* and other critical work.
MISCH, Georg. *A History of Autobiography in Antiquity.*
MORLEY, John. *Life of Gladstone.*
MURRAY, Katharine. *Caught in the Web of Words.*
NEW ENGLAND TOWN STUDIES. E.g., those of Lockridge, Demos, Greven and Gross.
NEWMAN, John Henry. *Apologia. . . .*
** NICOLSON, Harold. *The Development of English Biography, et al.*
OLNEY, James, ed. *Autobiography: Essays Theoretical and Critical, Metaphors of Self: The Meaning of Autobiography.*
** PACHTER, Marc. ed., *Telling Lives.*
PARKER, William Riley. On Milton.
PIPER, David. on the English face.
PLATO. *Phaedrus.*
RAYFIELD, Donald. *The Dream of Lhasa.*

Rosengarten, Theodore. *All God's Dangers: The Life of Nate Shaw.*
RUCKTÄSCHLE, Anna Maria and ZIMMERMANN Hans Dieter. eds., *Trivialliteratur*, especially Michael Kienzle's essay on Biography.
RULE, J. C. *Louis XIV and the Craft of Kingship.*
** SARTRE, Jean Paul. Especially on Flaubert.
SCHNEIDER, Manfred. on Heine's politics.
SCHOENBAUM, Samuel. *Shakespeare's Lives.*
SCHORER, Mark. on Sinclair Lewis.
SCHEUER, Helmut. *Biographie.*
SEWALL, Richard. on Emily Dickenson.
SHAKESPEARE, William. especially the histories and tragedies.
SKARISBRICK, J. B. *Henry VIII.*
SKINNER, Quentin. on Bolingbroke.
SLATER, Miriam. on the Verney family, and other family studies.
SOLZHENITSYN, Aleksandr. *August 1914.*
SPENCE, Jonathan. on Chinese figures.
STANNARD, David. Related writing especially Freudian criticism of biography.
STAUFFER, Donald A. on Biography.
STEELE, Ronald. *Walter Lippman and the American Century.*
*** STRACHEY, Lytton. *Eminent Victorians,* prefaces, and *obiter dicta.*
SULLOWAY, Frank J. on Freud.
SWEIG, Stefan. Related writing.
TERKEL, Studs. Related writing.
THOMPSON, Paul. *The Edwardians.*
TOLSTOY, Leo. *Childhood, Boyhood, Youth.*
TROYAT, Henri. *Tolstoy.*
TUCHMAN, Barbara (especially on Strauss and Germany in *The Proud Towers*).
UA RATHAILE.
* WATERS. on the Otis family, and other family studies.
WEISHEIPL, James A. *Friar Thomas d'Aquino.*
WIMSATT, W. K. on Pope's portraits.
WOLFF, Geoffrey. *The Duke of Deception.*
** WOOLF, Virginia. Spoofs: *Flush, Orlando,* and the novels. *Granite and Rainbow.*
ZLOBIN, Vladimir. *Zinaida Gippius.*

C. Biography as a Force in Cultural and Intercultural Affairs.

The following is a summary of the major points made by those answering questions 3, 4, 5 and 6 on the questionnaire.

Different nations and cultures produce different modes of biography. The most palpable differences are in the areas of philosophy, function and methodology.

(a) Philosophy, or doctrine, and function:

Most respondents emphasize this difference; they point out that each culture has different myths and ceremonies, and different notions of the hero to accord with these myths (Nikki Giovanni). The myths vary with different social, political and cultural circumstances (Edel). Many note here the difference between East and West (Prabhu Gupta-ra); between individual-centered versus group-centered societies (Manganyi); and especially recently, between Communist and Non-communist countries. Auty notes that biography tends to derive from, and reinforce, the cultural presuppositions of the state or group in which it is written, and that often, the epitomizing hero is used to boost national glory—whether the nation be "totalitarian" or "democratic."

Most responses came from the West. There was naturally a tendency to see the "democratic" countries as being less susceptible to social hagiography or distortion for political ends. (see also on "biography and social problems" below).

(b) Methodology:
Naturally the above was found to bear on biographical methods. The ample and relentless use of evidence is more important in the would-be-objective biography of the Western liberals than in that of countries producing "state biographies" (Colp). Sometimes the presuppositions of a society will appear to defeat biography entirely or to destroy its quality—India's "otherworldly" cast prior to the Muslim invasions (Guptara), for example, or the African emphasis on the community rather than on the individual (Manganyi). Illiteracy can also either inhibit or affect the state of the genre (Bradbrook).

An important point is the different attitudes which various societies have developed towards biography as an art. Merle finds it difficult to make comparisons between his nation and others because "systematic biographical studies don't exist in France." In Germany, biography is regarded as a form of *triviallitur* (Sammons). Many note America's seriousness in this matter of craft, and contrast the rigorous scholarship and exhaustive detail of U.S. biographies with the more casual practise in some other countries (Peters). There were those other than Americans who complimented the American writers on well-directed insights not always found elsewhere. Colin Brooks, for example, finds them more adventurous and often less "magisterial" than their British counterparts.

There is some, but not enough cross-cultural interchange among biographers. There has, say the respondents, been more rapport recently. Some demur; or say "very little." All agree that it's too little. These were the three predominant attitudes to question 5.

The capacity of biographers to help focus cross-cultural questions and dilemmas. Contributors had more to say here. Most agree that biographers are at least helpful in focussing on the social problems of individual nations. "Biography takes the discussion of current cultural and ethical problems into the concrete world, where the real choices are made" (Betty Glad). More specifically, biography is seen as an aid to the breaking down of taboos; to enlightened discussion of minority problems; and to social and cultural movements such as the emancipation of women (N. and J. MacKenzie).

Erlanger speaks for many when he says that biography *must* be of cultural importance because it often treats the men who make history: "l'histoire a été faite essentiellement par des hommes, et a subi les conséquences de leurs passions." Coming the other way, but to the same end, Sammons says that "good biography is *ipso facto* culturally constructive: the very discipline contributes to the cultural and ethical dilemmas of civilization."

Some noted that biography enables us to learn from the mistakes of great (and not-so-great) men (e.g., Duncan). This is partly connected with the capacity of the genre to involve and transcend the times. Gindin points out that the form "focusses on a career, on change and development. . . . the current utility of biography is metaphorical: the study of how someone else dealt with problems . . . similar . . . and different [from current problems] in a different time and space." Others noted that biography is central to the understanding of history (Colin Brooks), and that "it is also the history of our times" (Moraji Desai).

On the other hand, biographers snow us what is unique in our time: ". . . No past figures confronted nuclear war, overpopulation, earth destruction" (Colp). This explains, says Bloom, the appeal of the holocaust diaries, for example.

In conclusion, a warning from some with Alice Goldfarb Marquis: "it would be a mistake to use biography as some kind of tool or paradigm for raising moral issues. Each person's life is a separate story."

D. *Biography and Other Disciplines—Recent Developments.*

The summaries given below apply most to answers to questions 7 and 8—although obviously the matter pertains partly to the responses previously summarized. The respondents emphasize particularly the interaction with the social sciences and literature. Psychology, political science, history, literature, sociology, anthropology, zoology, geology and linguistics are emphasized—and in that order.

In general, respondents feel that there was a more generous interaction than in the past and that this interaction is a two-way matter. There are those who did not see much change, however; and some of this independence partly salutary in that it helps avoid special trades applying their own restricting terms: "beware the dead hand of expert jargon" (Holroyd).

To deal specifically with some of the fields mentioned:

1. *Psychology.* The overwhelming tribute to the Freudian impact has already been dealt with above. Manganyi points out the three major areas of interaction, and his list covers the field:

   (a) the theory of personality structure and development
   (b) systematic qualitative (clinical) and quantitative (statistical) approaches to the investigation of personality and
   (c) systematic conceptualization of the personality/social structure interface.

The interchange is strongly two-way here. Psychologists are learning much from biography and especially from autobiography. This is particularly true as psychology approaches the women's movement, where women's biography and autobiography can be of great help—although there is a problem with Freudian psychology being male-centered.

2. *Political Science.* Again, the impact of Marxism is specified above. Recently this has intensified and more useful in that the Marxist "has been struggling for a definition of the social construction of individual consciousness. This has been healthy biography, even when the Marxists have been "unfriendly to individual specificity" (Sammons).

3. *History.* The more recent emphasis on the importance of context has made biographers—especially but not exclusively historical biographers—more dependent on historians. And many historians have found biography valuable in dramatizing their field. There is an obvious symptom of interchange here in the recent increase in the number of family histories.

4. *Literature.* There is still of course the traditional impact of literature. Recent literary critics have helped biographers to be wary of equating the man and the work. Bradbrook says that the literary connection "reminds one of the necessary element of fiction in all biography." Most particularly, many note the rapport between the two fields which did not exist during the reign of the new critics.

5. *Sociology and anthropology.* These have given and profited in valuable ways. Merle cites Daniel Bertaux as saying that "biography has caused sociologists to renew from top to bottom sociological prac-

tice." Winslow puts in a negative note here: "in matters of style, use of jargon, for example, the influence on biography has been baleful."

6. *Anthropology, zoology.* These disciplines have increasingly enabled biographers (especially those with subjects and scientific disciplines) to deal with the field and/or with elements of a subject's life which otherwise may be lost in time.

7. *Linguistics.* The awareness of how a writer's style may reveal his personality has been much aided by the linguistic study (Peters).

E. *Biography and the Polemical Commitment.*

This matter is covered in the responses to question 9. The answers given may be divided under three heads: 1. No; 2. Yes; and 3. To some extent—and perhaps inevitably.

1. *Definitely not.* Most respondents believe that conformity to a given social or political theory is destructive to good biography: "such biographies are as dead as their subjects before they are written" (Edel). Many deplore the damage to objective truth. "The evidence comes first," says Pierson. And Auty warns against "the selection of facts to suit the author's preconceived theories." There is a conviction that the accidental biases are enough, without invoking intentional ones.

2. *Why not?* "You are obviously expecting a negative answer," says M. C. Bradbrook (we were not), "but this is a real question." And some answers justified her statement. Most of the "why nots" feel that social and political commitment is simply inevitable. There is a prevailing sentiment that the bias must be announced: Why not, says Peters, "as long as the biographer announces where, in the popular jargon, he or she is coming from. What disturbs me is that many biographers seem to have no theory at all—political, economic, metaphysical, psychological, sociological, historical, aesthetic."

3. *To some extent.* Many feel that a little commitment is a good thing; particularly if it doesn't produce serious distortion of the subject's life. A few replies distinguish between commitment and conformity, and argue that the former is good and the latter bad. The point is made that the choice of a subject will probably involve a certain amount of preconception (Birman).

F. *Biography and the Interrelation with Literature and History.*

Respondents perceive a strong interrelation between biography and history, and nearly as strong an interrelationship between biography and literature. They argue that one cannot understand a figure out of the context of his time. The question seems to be: ". . . how much history should be put into the biographies of both historical and literary figures. Is it possible to write a history of the life and times of so and so? How much of the history of the times is necessary to a full portrait of a literary figure?" (Auty). Pierson quotes Carlyle: "history is the essence of innumerable biographies."

Many see biography as a point of reconciliation between history and literature. In the hands of a good writer, a subject "can become a complex biographical symbol of a completed historical movement and a distinctive cultural milieu" (Thomas M. Curley). Looking at it from the other direction, "biography can help explain, illuminate, both history and literature."

The strongest reply to question 10 raises the question of methodology. Thomas S. Hines sees the essential form of biography as derived from history: interpretive, analytical *narrative,* so that "biographers *must* be trained as historians."

The question is raised by some as to the intent of the sinister phrase: "study of . . ." in this question. Holroyd says that it is fine for biography to be related to Literature, but not to *the study of* literature.

G. *Biography and Autobiography—Recent Changes in the Interrelationship.*

Many of the responses to question 11 were interested in distinguishing between the two genres rather than discussing their recent interrelationship. Peters argues that the differences between biography and autobiography are becoming more and more understood, at least by scholars. She mentions James Melville Cox's contention that "biography is conservative (it commemorates) and that autobiography is radical (it asserts)." Bloom, among others, argues that "biography uses the historian's techniques . . . autobiography is much closer to the novel (especially *bildungsroman*)."

On the other hand, many say that the two forms are related and are becoming more so. Colp believes all biography to be part autobiography—due to the guiding intrusion of the author for whom the biography is, in part, an act of self-expression. In this connection, Gindin cites the narrating biographer of Sartre's *Nausea* who complains of his subject: "I can understand why he lied to everyone else around him, but why did he lie to me?"

Biography is seen as profitting more and more from autobiography. This is part of "the increased awareness of the importance of all archival material" (Auty); especially diaries and tapes by public figures and official memoirs. There is even a tendency, say some, for biography to approach autobiography—some regret this—and for autobiographers such as Howard Mumford Jones to approach biography, or even history.

H. *Biography and Ghosts.*

Question 12 produced most unanimity. An overwhelming number of responses castigate the ghost-writer as a biographic hireling who is paid to present a flattering picture of his subject. Leon Edel describes ghosts as frauds—although he says that behind the fraud "certain facts emerge." Holroyd charitably compares him with a barrister putting his client's case. Very few responses tolerate the ghost-writer. The words of Ronald Duncan sum it up: "Ghosts should be exorcised."

I. *Biography: Criticism and Reviewing.*

The following list of criteria for good criticism and reviewing is taken from Phyllis Auty's response to question 13. It subsumes most of the points made by others. Additional criteria will be added below:

1. Was the person chosen a suitable subject for biography?

2. Have the full facts about the life been chosen and the appropriate sources for them used?

3. Have these facts been arranged in such a way as to convey a true portrait of the whole person? and with a proper balance between private and public person

4. Does the biography show the way in which the person evolved and became sufficiently important in a special field . . . to become a suitable subject for biography?

5. Does the biography relate the person to his/her background and times?

6. Does it assess the importance of the subject in his/her special field . . .?

7. Does it convey the real and whole human being, does it make him/her a living person, and is it a good read?

To this list we may add the suggestions of others that good criticism should relate the subjects crises or agonies to those of his time; that it should eschew mere summary; show an ability to establish the accuracy of the facts; assess the author's capacity to present his subject in a vital and dramatic way; and point out how well the author has shaped his material.

J. *Biography and Contemporary Values.*

Most find it fruitful to discuss the role of biography in assessing contemporary values. Many specify contemporary issues which they feel have benefitted from treatment in biographical or autobiographical writing: civil rights; women's liberation; sexual relations; child-parent relations and so forth.

Other respondents, however, don't agree. "Futile, utterly futile," answers Ruth Dudley Edwards. On a less absolute note, Bradbrook says that "it depends on who's doing the discussing."

K. *Biography as a Distinct Discipline.*

Most of the respondents to question 15 say that biography is not a distinct discipline. It is termed "a sub-discipline: *literae humaniores*"; a highly specialized branch of history (Edel and others); a profitably amorphous discipline (Holroyd); a profession rather than a discipline; and an art.

There were some who disagree with his verdict. Bloom asserts that it is a variegated form, but one with distinct and assessable characteristics. Others say it is as distinct as any discipline, but more difficult to codify.

L. *Biography: Future Directions.*

There was a great richness of speculation in the answers to the last question. Many of the suggestions had to do with facilities. Auty and others call for specialized research centers for the use of biographers. These should be equipped with libraries, tape facilities, data banks, and all the technical aids which are of especial use to biographers.

Other directions pertain to the content of future biographies: more treatment of women; more concern with world issues; more frank discussion of certain social and personal problems *etc.*

But most of the speculation concerned form and craft. Manganyi foresees more joint works treating interdisciplinary figures or groups. Holroyd thinks it likely that there will be more woman writers who will do for biography what women novelists did for the novel. Other proposed developments include: group biography; the biography of the common man; biography which mixes historical figures with fictional ones—as in Solzhenitsyn's *August, 1914;* and *avant garde* biography employing such devices as have long been used by novelists— stream of consciousness; authorial uncertainty; collage and so on. The future of biography, it seems, will be a profuse one!

Summarized by ANTHONY FRIEDSON

Index

Notes on the Authors

Phyllis Auty received her M.A. and B.Litt. from Oxford. During World War II, she worked with the B.B.C. and the British Foreign Office, serving in the Middle East and Italy. After the war, Professor Auty worked for UNRRA and has visited Yugoslavia frequently since 1945. She is well-known as a writer on Yugoslav history and on modern Yugoslavia. She has worked on the biographies of Prince Paul of Yugoslavia and of James Bouchier, Balkan correspondent of *The Times* before World War I. Her best known work to date is her *Tito: A Biography* (1970). Professor Auty was a Reader in South Slav history from 1950 to 1974, and has held other academic posts. She is currently writing on Tito and Churchill.

Leon Edel was educated at McGill University and the University of Paris. Interrupting a career in journalism and broadcasting, he served in the U.S. Army during World War II. In 1950 he joined the faculty at New York University and eventually became Henry James Professor of English Letters there. In 1972, he was appointed Citizens' Professor of English at the University of Hawaii. Among Professor Edel's many awards and honors are the 1963 Pulitzer Prize and the 1963 National Book Award for *The Life of Henry James*. This five-volume work is perhaps his best-known biography. Among his many other works are *The Psychological Novel* (1965), *Literary Biography* (1957), *Henry D. Thoreau* (1970), and *Bloomsbury: A House of Lions* (1979). Professor Edel is editor of the Edmund Wilson papers.

Michael Holroyd studied science at Eton and read literature at his local library at Maidenhead. From 1973 to 1974 he was Chairman of the Society of Authors in Britain and from 1976 to 1978 Chairman of the National Book League. In 1979 he was Visiting Fellow at the Institute for Arts and Humanistic Studies in Pennsylvania State University. He was awarded the Saxton Memorial Fellowship in 1964; a Bollingen Fellowship in 1966; and a Winston Churchill Fellowship in 1971. He is a Fellow of the Royal Historical Society and a Fellow of the Royal Society of Literature (of whose Council he is a member). Among Mr. Holroyd's best known works are biographies of *Hugh Kingsmill* (1964), *Lytton Strachey* (2 vols.; 1967–68), and *Augustus John* (1975). In addition to his books he has contributed to many British and American periodicals; lectured widely in both countries; and written scripts for television and radio. He is presently working on the authorized biography of Bernard Shaw.

Noel Chabani Manganyi was born in South Africa. He took his D. Litt. et Phil. in psychology, and interned in clinical psychology at Baragwanath Hospital in Johannesburg in 1969. He was a post-doctoral Fellow in Clinical Psychology at Yale University School of Medicine, Department of Psychiatry, from 1973 to 1975. In 1976 Professor Manganyi became Chairman of the Department of Psychology at the University of Transkei. The author of numerous conference papers and scholarly articles, Professor Manganyi has also published *Being Black in the World* (1973), *Alienation and the Body in Racist Society* (1977), *Mashangu's Reverie* (1977), and *Looking through the Keyhole: Dissenting Essays on the Black Experience* (1981). Professor Manganyi is Senior Research Fellow at the African Studies Institute, University of Witwatersrand and is currently engaged in researching the life and work of the South African writer and critic Ezekiel Mphahlele.

Gabriel Merle was trained in both French and English literature, and this dual interest culminated in his receiving his Doctorat d'État from the English department of the Sorbonne for a thesis on Lytton Strachey. He was later appointed Professor, and is now chairman of his department, at Université Paris VII. Professor Merle has published in literature, pedagogy, and administration. His special interest in linguistics has prompted him to write on the style of Lytton Strachey and others. His *Lytton Strachey: Biography and Critique of a Critic and Biographer* was published this year.

Margot Peters was born in Wisconsin, and took her Ph.D. from the University of Wisconsin at Madison. She is currently Professor of English at the University of Wisconsin-Whitewater. Her primary publications are *Charlotte Brontë: Style in the Novel* (1973), *Unquiet Soul: A Biography of Charlotte Brontë* (1975), and *Bernard Shaw and the Actresses* (1980); she has written numerous essays on Shaw, Brontë, women's studies, biography, and detective fiction. In 1975 *Unquiet Soul* won the Friends of American Writers' cash award for the best work of prose; in

1976–77 Professor Peters held a Fellowship from the American Council of Learned Societies; in 1978 she was Kathe Tappe Vernon Professor of Biography at Dartmouth College. She is currently working on a biography of Mrs. Patrick Campbell, and has just completed *Sherlock Holmes and the Ibsen Contingent* (1980).

Shoichi Saeki was born in Tokyo, but grew up in the "Japanese Alps" of north-central Japan. He studied American Literature at Tokyo University and graduated during World War II. His academic career was interrupted by two years' service in the Japanese Navy. After the war he resumed his literary career; taught English at Tokyo Municipal University and, from 1968 to the present, at Tokyo University. He has also taught Japanese literature at various American universities. Early in his career, Professor Saeki began to write critical articles for the literary magazines and newspapers and did some translations. His *Notes on the Contemporary American Novel* (1956) was followed by many other works. Those concerned with biographical studies are: *Between Biography and Criticism* (1967), *Yukio Mishima: Critical Biography* (1978), *I Wrote, Loved, and Lived: A Biography of Ernest Hemingway* (1979), and *Japanese Autobiographies* (1975). In 1980, Professor Saeki was awarded the Yomiuri Literary Prize for *Narrative Art in Modern Japan*, and the Translator's Prize for the translation of Tony Tanner's *City of Words*.

DATE DUE			

New directions ...   183214